PHOTOGRAPHY Tutorial and Workbook

KIMBERLY R. NORTON

Please send Errors, Corrections, Omissions, and/or Suggestions to:

Kimberly Norton
krn@usa.com

©2013 BY KIMBERLY R. NORTON
ALL RIGHTS RESERVED

ISBN-13: 978-1494927943
ISBN-10: 1494927942

DISCLAIMER
EFFORTS HAVE BEEN TAKEN TO ENSURE THE CONTENTS OF THIS BOOK ARE CORRECT. I AM ONLY HUMAN AND HUMANS MAKE MISTAKES. THE AUTHOR NOR THE PUBLISHER OF THIS BOOK WILL BE HELD LIABLE FOR THE USE, OR MISUSE, OF THE CONTENTS IN THIS BOOK.

Contents

INTRODUCTION 5

METERING 9

APERTURE 15

SHUTTER SPEED 31

PROGRAM MODE 59

ISO SENSITIVITY 63

EXPOSURE 77

EXPOSURE COMPENSATION 87

BRACKETING 99

HISTOGRAM 111

WHITE BALANCE 123

CUSTOM WHITE BALANCE 133

MANUAL MODE 141

LONG EXPOSURE 149

ASPECT RATIO 157

SENSOR SIZE 167

LIGHT 171

CAMERA RAW on JPEGS 179

INDEX 185

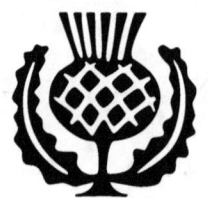

INTRODUCTION

This book assumes you know how to use a camera in AUTO mode. Therefore I will not go into all the details of what a camera is and how a camera is made. The focus of this book is strictly on moving away from point and shoot techniques and moving toward manual controls.

Before going any farther let's get one important question out of the way.

What is a photograph?

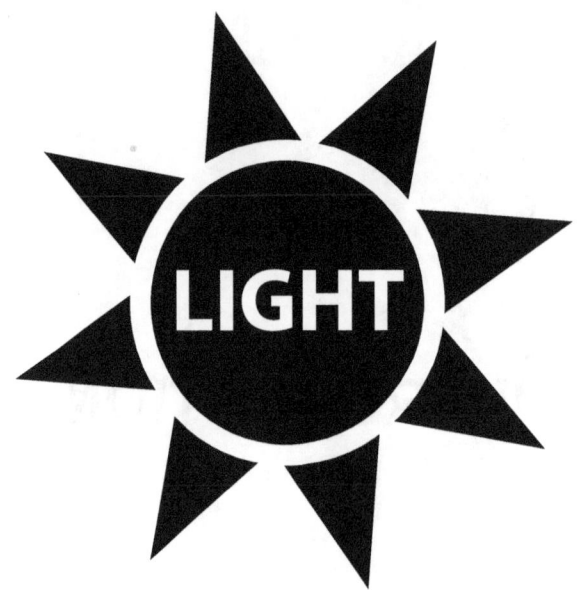

A photograph is light, light, and more light

In more specific terms, a photograph is a drawing made of light. As you move toward using manual controls you will learn how to double the amount of light entering the camera and how to halve the amount of light entering the camera. This doubling and halving is accomplished through exposure.

What is Exposure?
Exposure is a constant amount of **LIGHT** entering the camera. Exposure is accomplished by using **MAPS** and **ISO**. We will cover exposure in detail later.

What is MAPS?
MAPS is the acronym for **M**anual, **A**perture priority, **P**rogram mode, and **S**hutter Speed priority. Most cameras have these items listed as M, A, S, P, which I use to create the acronym MAPS. When dealing with MAPS we will double the light entering the camera or cut the light in half entering the camera. Please note that some cameras use TV (time value) instead of **S**, and AV (aperture value) instead of **A**. We will learn about MAPS in the sections to come.

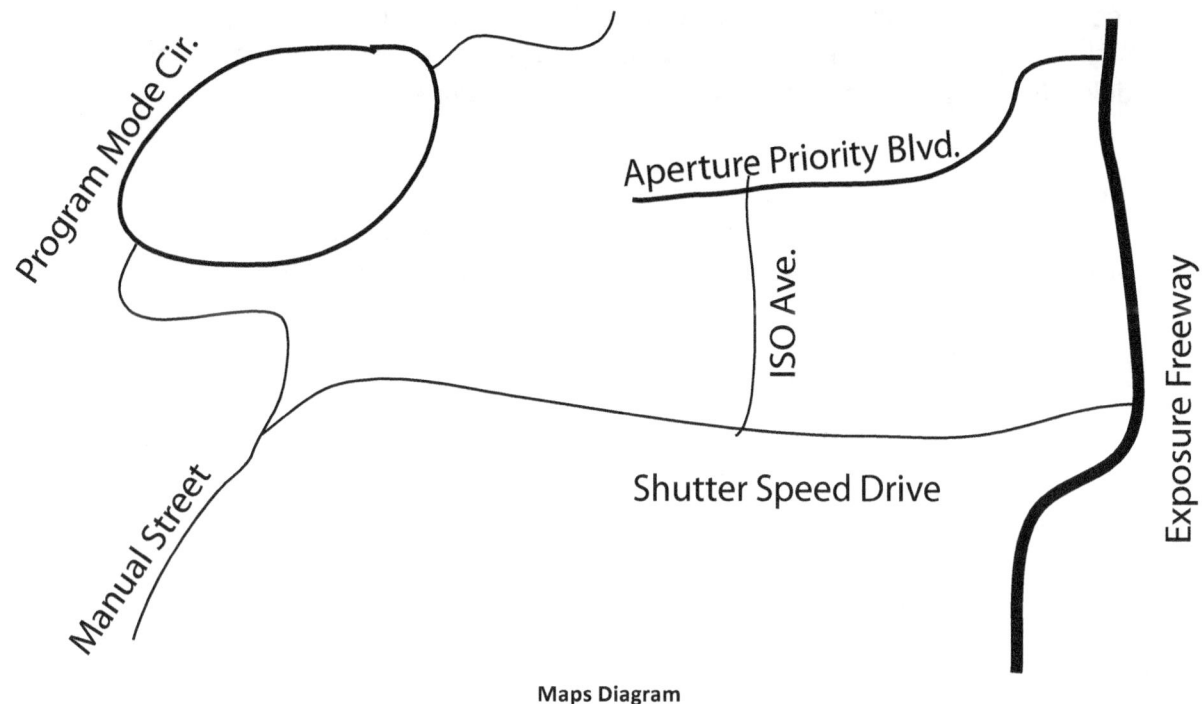

Maps Diagram

What is ISO?
ISO is a numerical value indicating your camera's sensitivity to light. We will learn about ISO in the sections to come.

Assignments
As a general rule, there will be two assignments on each section. I will work the first assignment appended with the wording "in Action". You will work the second assignment which will closely resemble the "in Action" assignment. I recommend that you scan through the "in Action" assignment until you get the gist of what is going on. Everything will make more sense to you when you actually work your own assignment, so please do not be discouraged if you do not understand the "in Action" assignment.

Once you begin work on your assignment, you should stay with it until you completely understand the concepts. If you cannot get your assignment to work correctly then stick with it and make notes on what you did or did not do. It may take you about three tries before getting your assignment to work correctly.

Just reading the book will not help you. The student must actually work the assignments. Working the assignments is the only way to become proficient with using manual controls on your camera.

When answering questions, be sure to include the name of your camera, like Nikon d7100, or Sony RX100, and so on.

Image Quality
Feel free to use the lowest image quality possible to complete your assignments as doing so will save on ink cost from your personal printer. Also note that the images taken in this book have been created with the lowest settings possible.

Tools needed
Great care has been taken to ensure the student can use common household items for their projects. The tools needed throughout this book are as follows:

- Can goods (qty. 3)
- Deck of cards, only 3 cards need
- Yellow highlighter
- Fan, or optional ceiling fan
- Printer
- Scissors
- Tape or glue
- Camera
- Tripod
- Camera user guide

METERING

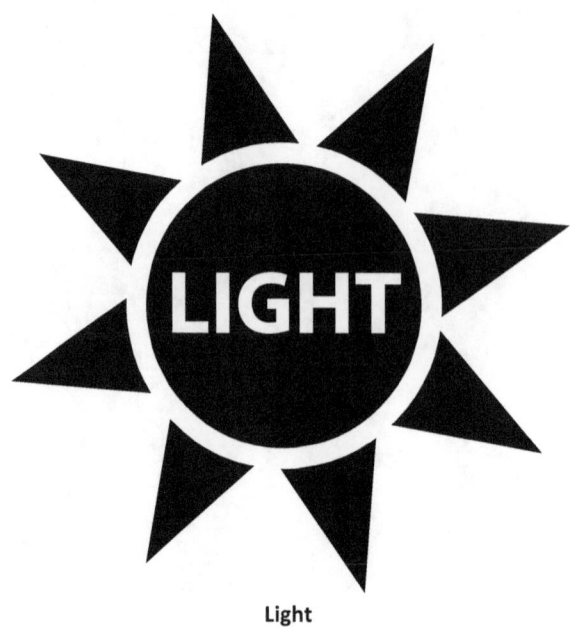
Light

A photograph is made of light. The way your camera computes that light is done through a process called **metering**. With metering, the camera takes a **light** reading of its surroundings then computes the correct **exposure** (covered later) for a scene.

Many digital cameras will offer three types of metering (**light** readings), namely, Matrix, Center-weighted, and Spot. With these different types of metering, the photographer tells the camera how light is supposed to be measured.

Metering might sound complicated yet it is quite easy. You as a photographer select one of three metering options below and the camera does the rest!

Matrix metering
The camera meters a wide area of the frame then sets exposure accordingly. This is the default metering on the Nikon d7100. The Canon 7d lists this type of metering as **Evaluative metering**.

Center-weighted metering
The camera meters the entire frame of the scene but gives more weight to the center of the frame.

Spot metering
The camera meters a certain spot where the focus is located. This is a great choice when you need an accurate exposure of a very small portion of your frame.

If the photographer does not set a specific type of meter then the camera's metering system will be set with the manufacturer's default value. Please note that different camera manufactures use different names for metering.

METERING IN ACTION

Tools needed:
    Camera
    User Manual

Things to Note
Metering is usually done before doing **Exposure Compensation** and before **Bracketing**. Those two concepts will be covered later.

STEPS for Metering in Action

1. Document how to change your camera's metering mode:

On the Nikon D7100, press the Metering button at the top right of the camera (the Metering button has five dots on it). Rotate the Main command dial until the desired meter is selected.

2. Set your camera's meter to **Matrix** (or equivalent).
3. Draw an image of that icon. Write the icon's name used by the manufacturer.

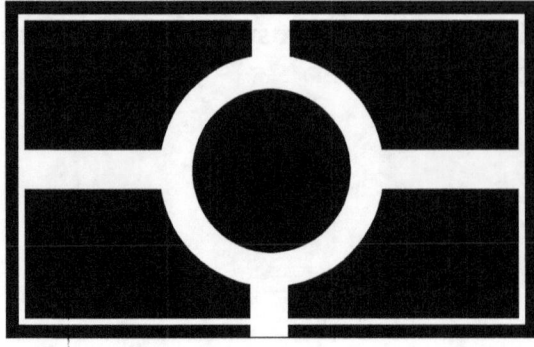

Matrix

4. Set your camera's meter to **Center weighted** (or equivalent).
5. Draw an image of that icon. Write the icon's name used by the manufacturer.

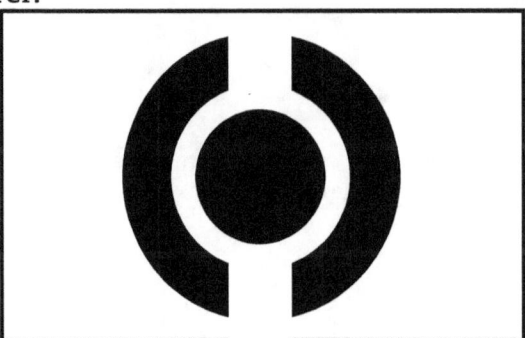

Center-weighted

6. Set your camera's meter to **Spot** (or equivalent).
7. Draw an image of that icon. Write the icon's named use by the manufacturer.

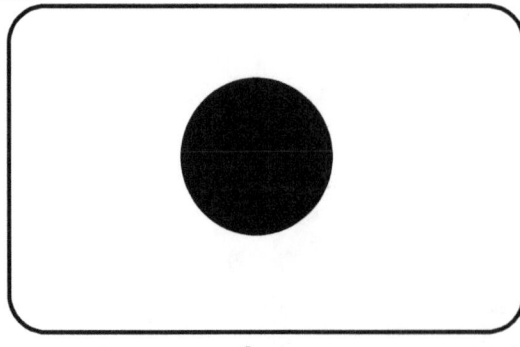

Spot

METERING ASSIGNMENT

Tools needed:
    Camera
    User Manual

Things to Note
Metering is usually done before doing **Exposure Compensation** and before **Bracketing**. Those two concepts will be covered later.

STEPS for Metering Assignment

1. **Document how to change your camera's metering mode:**

2. Set your camera's meter to **Matrix** (or equivalent).
3. Draw an image of that icon. Write the icon's name used by the manufacturer.

4. Set your camera's meter to **Center weighted** (or equivalent).
5. Draw an image of that icon. Write the icon's name used by the manufacturer.

6. Set your camera's meter to **Spot** (or equivalent).
7. Draw an image of that icon. Write the icon's name used by the manufacturer.

APERTURE

The **aperture** is an opening in the **lens** that determines the amount of light entering through the lens. Aperture is denoted with **f stops** (also known as **f** numbers).

The smaller the f number the larger the **area** of the aperture. The larger the f number the smaller the **area** of the aperture. So f1.4 has a wider **area** than f8. Or we can say, f stop 1.4 has a wider area than f stop 8.

Below is a depiction of the wideness of the aperture while using the **stairs diagram**. When decreasing the aperture (larger f numbers) you are going down stairs and it is known as **stopping down** (or **stepping down**). When increasing the aperture (small f numbers) you are going up stairs and it is known as **opening up** the aperture.

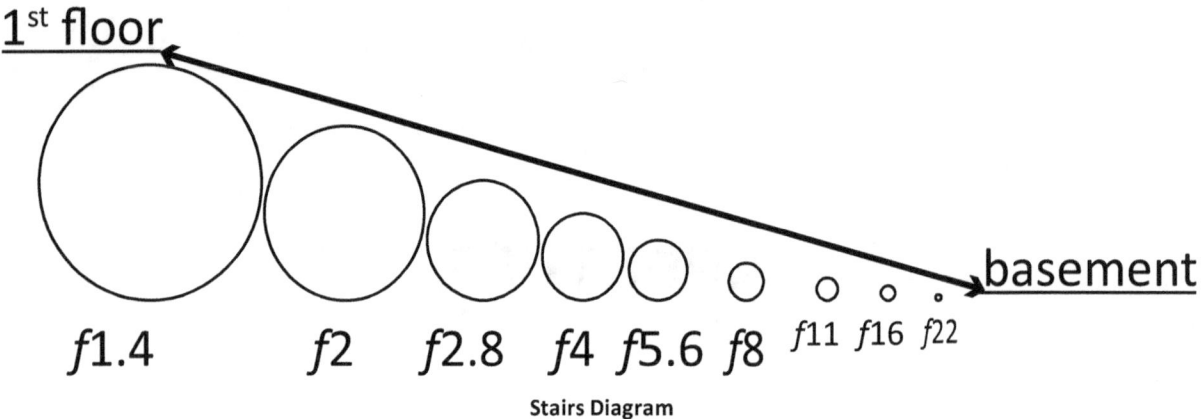

Stairs Diagram

On the stairs diagram, you are on the first step of the first floor (f1.4). As you step down toward the basement, the area under the steps becomes smaller (see the circles) but the **number of steps** you have to take **increases**. In the above diagram you actually take a total of **9** physical steps to get to the basement. Please note that each step is a full stop in photography terms, hence, the numbers are not sequential from one to nine. Move one stop to the left (toward the 1st floor), and you double the light entering the camera. Move a stop to the right (toward the basement), and you halve the light entering the camera.

1st floor		basement
More Light		Less Light
Wider Aperture		Smaller Aperture
Fast Lens		Slow Lens
Opening up lens		Stopping down lens
⬅———————————————————➡		
Smaller f number		Larger f number
Less Depth of Field		More depth of Field
Portrait shots		Landscape shots

Aperture

16

When you take a portrait of someone and you only want the person's face to be in focus then you open up the lens and have what is called a wide aperture (less depth of field). This concept is known as **Bokeh**. When light enters a wide aperture lens, the light scatters and bounces around causing the non focused area to be soft with a blurred look.

When taking photos of landscape objects you will usually stop down the lens to make sure everything is in focus (more depth of field).

Some lenses will list max apertures as in the following: **18-140mm f/3.5-5.6 zoom**.

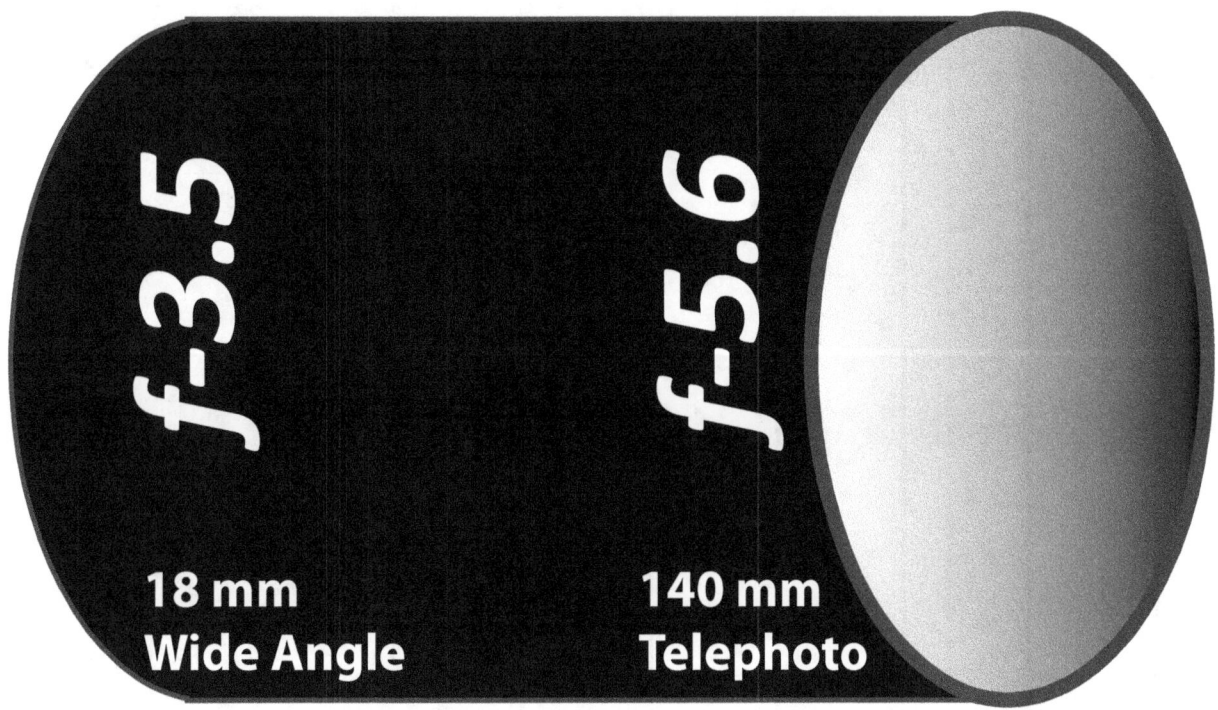

Zoom Lens

The numbers 18-140 mean the lens can zoom from 18mm (wide angle) to 140mm (telephoto). Any number between (and including the endpoints) 18-140 is considered to be a focal length. If the lens is zoomed to 70mm then it has a focal length of 70mm. If the lens is zoomed to 100mm then it has a focal length of 100mm.

The f/3.5-5.6 means the widest aperture of f3.5 is obtained at the 18mm end, but at the 140mm end the widest the aperture that can be obtained is only **f**5.6. Therefore, when zoomed all the way in at 140mm, you cannot open the aperture up to f3.5 as the widest you can get is f5.6. As you will see later, the aperture of this lens can step down to much larger numbers than f-5.6, but it cannot step up to smaller numbers than f-3.5. In essence, **f** notation on a lens depicts how wide the aperture can be (big hole but small f number), but it does not indicate how shallow an aperture can be (small hole but big f number).

Note: When the aperture is set to f3.5, on this lens, the lens is said to be **wide open**.

F-STOPS

The stairs diagram is based on FULL STOPS. Some cameras also offer one half stops and one third stops. The diagram below list some of the different stop values one might encounter.

Light	Width	Speed	Opening	f#	DOF	Full stops	½ stops	1/3 stops
More light	Wider Aperture	Fast Lens	Opening up	Smaller *f* number	Less Depth of Field	*f*2.8	2.8	2.8
↑	↑	↑	↑	↑	↑			3.2
							3.3	
								3.5
						*f*4	4	4
								4.5
							4.8	
								5
						*f*5.6	5.6	5.6
								6.3
							6.7	
								7.1
						*f*8	8	8
								9
							9.5	
								10
						*f*11	11	11
								13
							13	
								14
						*f*16	16	16
								18
							19	
								20
↓	↓	↓	↓	↓	↓	*f*22	22	22
Less light	Smaller Aperture	Slow Lens	Stopping down	Larger *f* number	More Depth of Field			

F-Stops

When stopping down ONE stop from f2.8 to f4 you are halving the amount of light entering the camera's image sensor. When opening up ONE stop from f4 to f2.8 you are doubling the amount of light entering the camera's image sensor.

APERTURE PRIORITY MODE
Most cameras contain an aperture priority mode. When a camera is in aperture priority mode, the user sets the aperture value and the camera automatically sets the correct **shutter spee**d (covered later). Aperture Priority is the **A** in our acronym **MAPS**.

In the next section, **Aperture Priority in Action**, you will see photographs taken with the Nikkor 18-140mm f/3.5-5.6 lens which is zoomed in to 70mm. When this lens is zoomed to 70mm then the max aperture is f5. If I want to open the aperture up to f3.5 I will have to zoom out to 18mm. If you do not understand this concept then do not worry about it. The concept will make more sense once you begin your assignment.

When you start your aperture priority assignment, your beginning f number and ending f number may be different from mine as the f number is dependent on the type of lens used and the focal length you chose to set your lens at.

Other considerations is whether the lens is in auto focus mode or manual mode. In many cases you will not get the desired results trying to use auto focus when working in aperture priority mode. As a result, the assignments require manually focusing the camera lens.

APERTURE PRIORITY IN ACTION

Tools needed:
    Dolls (3)
    Can goods (3)
    Yellow highlighter
    Camera
    Tripod
    User guide

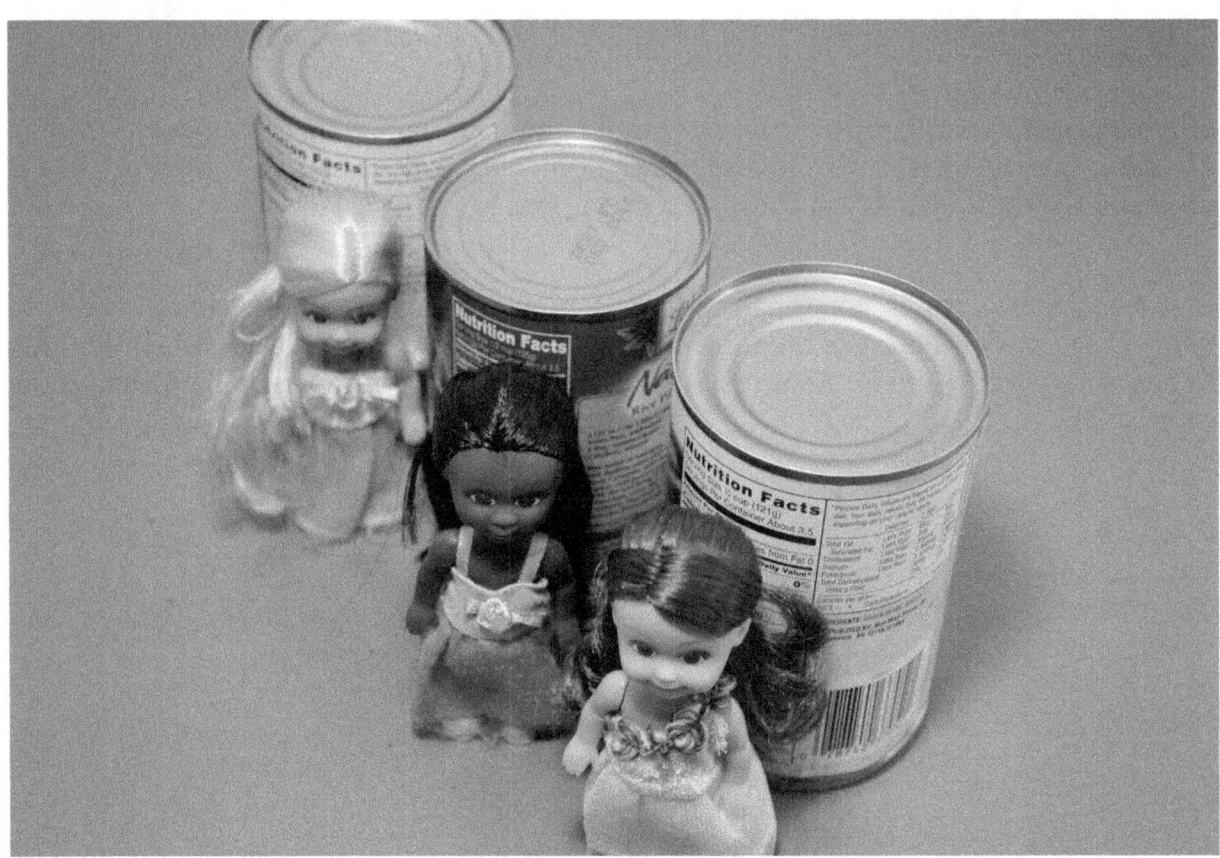

Aperture Priority Doll Setup

ACCESSING IMAGE INFORMATION

This assignment will require accessing image information. To access the F number, Exposure time, ISO, and Focal Length, do the following:

- **MAC**: right click the file, select *Get Info*, then click the down arrow under *More Info*. You will need your camera's software to see the ISO settings on a MAC.
- **PC**: right click the file, select *Properties*, click the *Details* tab, scroll down to Camera.

Things to Note
The aperture value will change as the lens's focal length changes. At the widest angle of the lens I have the fullest aperture possible (f3.5). When I zoom in, the aperture decreases in size giving a larger f number (f5).

STEPS for Aperture Priority in Action

1. **Document how to access your camera's Aperture Priority settings:**

On the Nikon D7100: Turn on the camera. Press the Mode dial lock release then turn the <u>Mode dial to A</u>, aligning the A up with the white dot. Rotate the <u>Sub Command dial</u> on the front of the camera to the right to step down the aperture (bigger f numbers) and to the left to open up the aperture (smaller f numbers). If the aperture values disappear before you make a selection, then press the Metering button at the top right of the camera (the Metering button has five dots on it).

2. **Document how to Manually Focus your Lens:**

On the Nikon D7100: Move the Focus-Mode selector to M. The Focus-Mode selector is on the front of the camera and has the letters AF and M stamped above it. To manually focus the lens, adjust the lens's focusing ring until the image is clear. The focusing ring is behind the zoom area of the lens.

3. Place three **cans** side by side. Move the left can backward and right can forward.
4. Place each **doll** against a can.
5. Place camera on a **tripod** and zoom all the way out (wide angle).
6. Open up to the widest aperture.
7. **Manually** focus on the center doll.
8. What is your **focal length?** 18mm
9. What is your **f value?** f3.5
10. Zoom your lens in to get a closer shot of the three dolls.
11. Open up to the widest aperture again.
12. **Manually** focus on the center doll.
13. What is your **focal length?** 70mm
14. What is its **new f value?** f5
15. Do not change your focal length nor refocus for the rest of this assignment.
16. Starting with the **widest aperture** (answer from question 14) and stepping down to the **smallest aperture** (largest f number) snap a photo of the dolls at each aperture step, half step, or third step.
17. Print, Cut, and Paste the widest aperture in the top box and the smallest aperture in the bottom box on the next page.
18. Document your findings, of both images, below that image.
19. Document the **File name, F number, Exposure time, ISO,** and **Focal Length**, of each image.
20. **Highlight** the Full Stops on the Image Information page using a marker.
21. **Overview**: Explain in your own words what is happening based on the image information data (and photos) plus draw a diagram showing aperture numbers vs. sizes. Make sure to underline key words and concepts.

WIDEST AND SMALLEST APERTURES

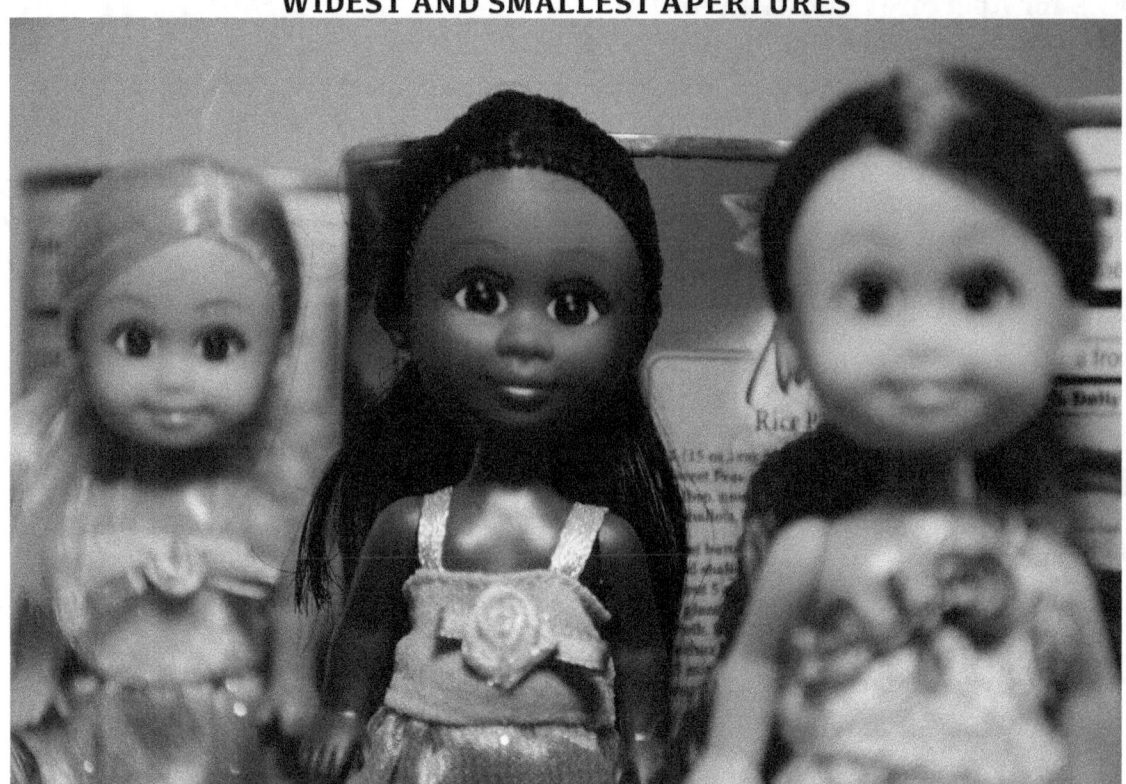

Aperture Priority f5

At the widest aperture f5 (smallest f number), the center doll, where I was focusing, is clear. The two outside dolls are blurry. This is called a shallow depth of field, the lens was opened up allowing more light to enter.

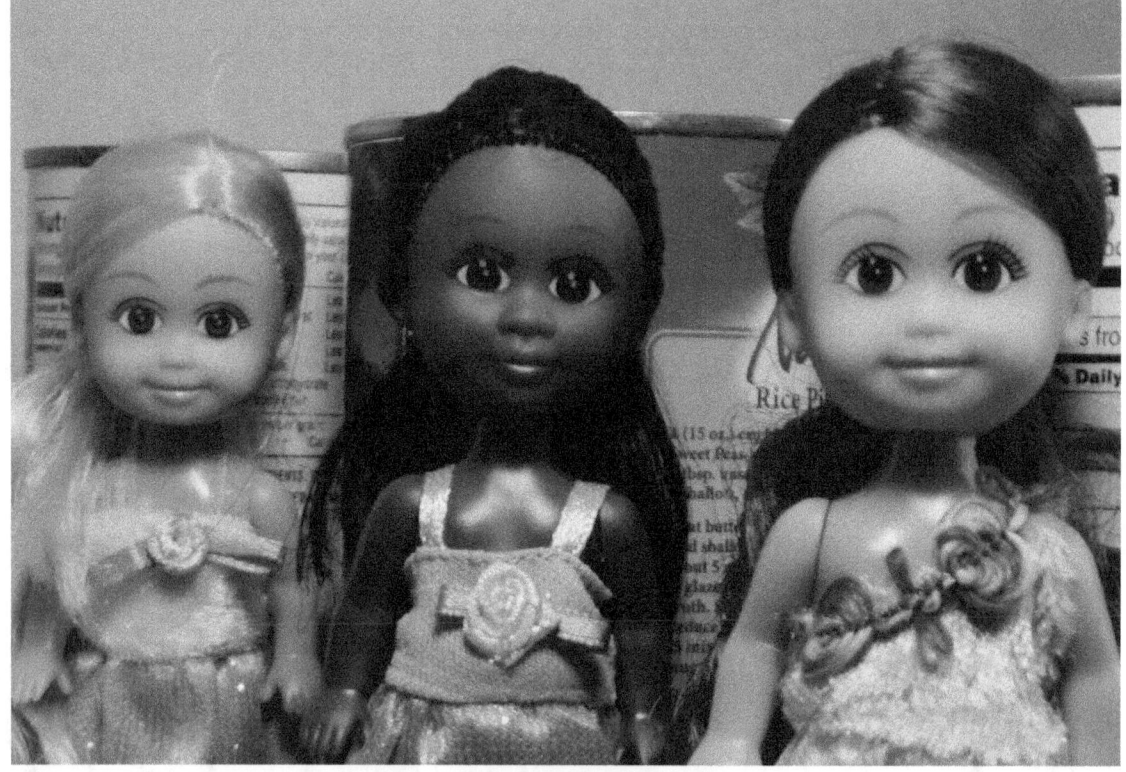

Aperture Priority f32

At the smallest aperture f32 (larger f number) all the dolls are in focus although I only focused on the center doll. This is known as more depth of field, the lens is stopped down allowing less light to enter.

IMAGE INFORMATION

File name	F-Number	Exposure Time (Shutter Speed)	ISO	Focal Length
DSC_0232.jpg	f5	1/30s	100	70mm
DSC_0233.jpg	f5.6	1/25s	100	70mm
DSC_0234.jpg	f6.3	1/20s	100	70mm
DSC_0235.jpg	f7.1	1/15s	100	70mm
DSC_0236.jpg	f8	1/13s	100	70mm
DSC_0237.jpg	f9	1/10s	100	70mm
DSC_0238.jpg	f10	1/8s	100	70mm
DSC_0239.jpg	f11	1/6s	100	70mm
DSC_0240.jpg	f13	1/5s	100	70mm
DSC_0241.jpg	f14	1/4s	100	70mm
DSC_0242.jpg	f16	1/3s	100	70mm
DSC_0243.jpg	f18	1/2.5s	100	70mm
DSC_0244.jpg	f20	1/2s	100	70mm
DSC_0245.jpg	f22	1/1.6s	100	70mm
DSC_0246.jpg	f25	1/1.3s	100	70mm
DSC_0247.jpg	f29	1s	100	70mm
DSC_0248.jpg	f32	1.3s	100	70mm

You may not need all the squares listed

OVERVIEW

At the widest aperture, the smallest number of f5, the center doll was in focus but the other dolls were out of focus. This means we had <u>less (a shallow) depth of field</u> at the widest aperture. As the <u>aperture decreased</u>, meaning larger f numbers, then all dolls became in focus which is known as <u>more depth of field</u>.

From f5, I <u>stepped down 1/3rd of a stop</u> to f5.6. Note that F5.6 is a 1/3rd stop, a half stop, and a full stop.

As the aperture decreases (gets a smaller hole with a larger f number) the Exposure time becomes longer. For example, at f5, the shutter opens and closes in one-thirtieth of a second (1/30th Sec). At f29, it takes a whole second for the shutter to open and close. At f32, it takes over a second (1.3 sec) to open and close the shutter. Hence, if we decrease the aperture's width (larger f number) the shutter speed (Exposure time) will increase in the amount of time it stays open. This can also be said as, when we <u>stop down</u>, the shutter takes longer to open and close. When we <u>open up</u>, the shutter opens and closes faster. As the aperture's width decreases, the speed of the shutter also decreases (which means the amount of time the shutter stays open increases).

Wide Aperture (small f number) = faster opening and closing of shutter.
Small Aperture (large f number) = slower opening and closing of shutter.

The focal length stays constant at a 70mm zoom since I did not refocus the lens. This ISO remains constant at 100 since it was not changed.

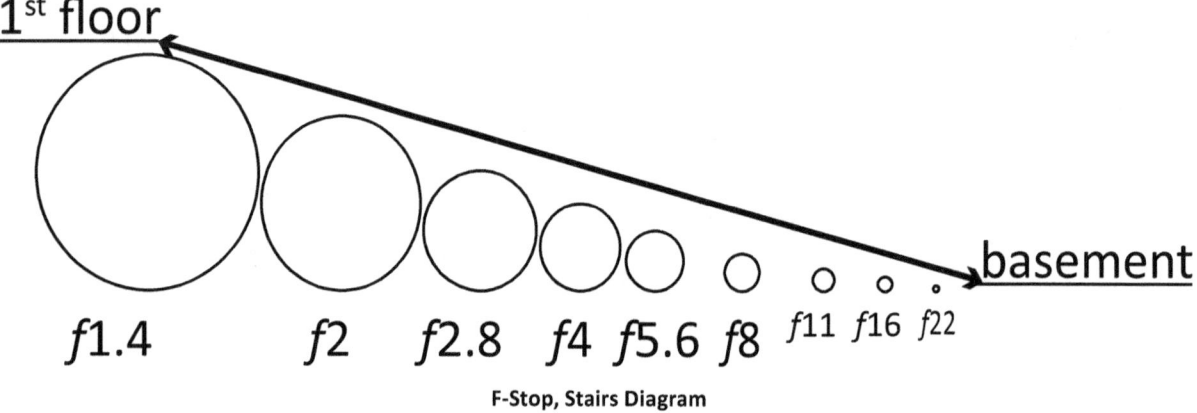

F-Stop, Stairs Diagram

APERTURE PRIORITY ASSIGNMENT

Tools needed:
    Deck of Cards (3 individual cards)
    Can goods (3)
    Yellow highlighter
    Camera
    Tripod
    User guide

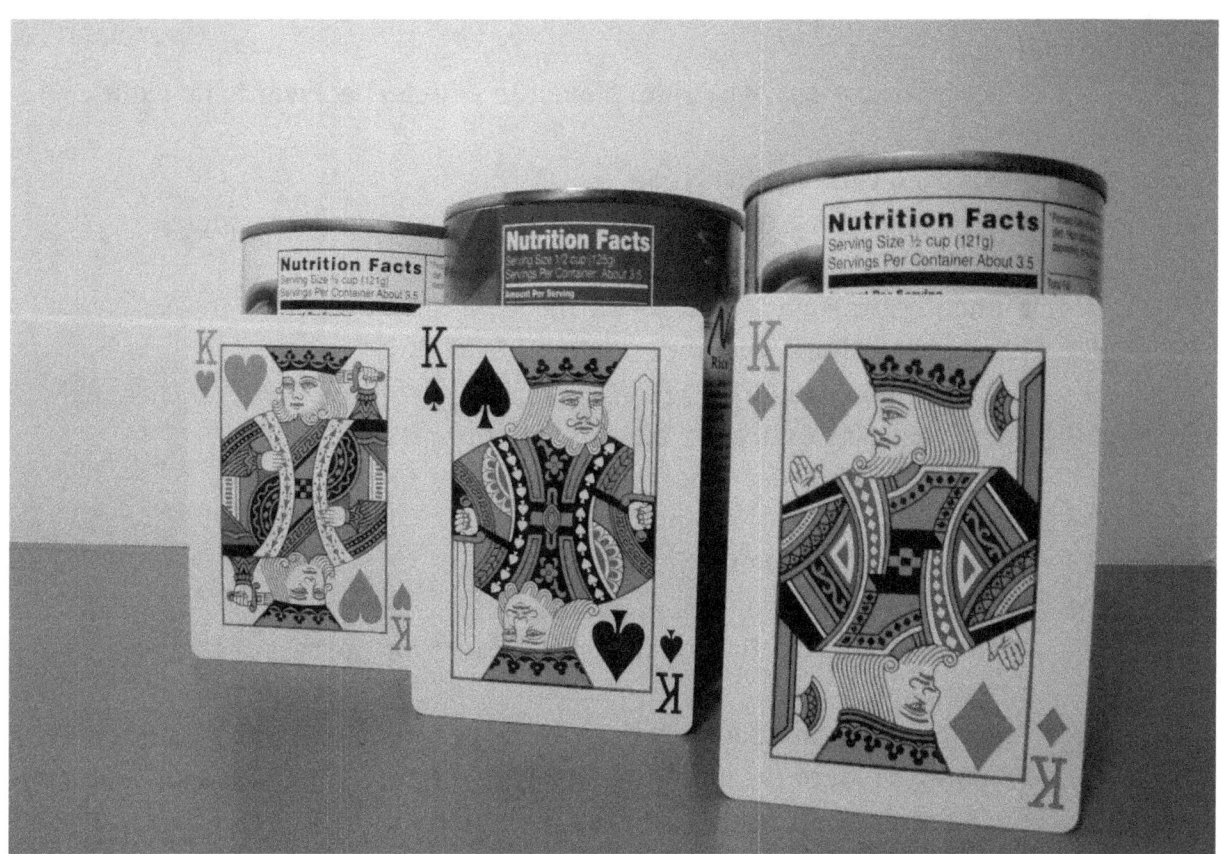

Aperture Priority Card Location

If at any time you need help with this assignment then refer to the **Aperture Priority in Action** section.

ACCESSING IMAGE INFORMATION
This assignment will require accessing image information. To access the F number, Exposure time, ISO, and Focal Length, do the following:

- **MAC**: right click the file, select *Get Info*, then click the down arrow under *More Info*. You will need your camera's software to see the ISO settings on a MAC.
- **PC**: right click the file, select *Properties*, click the *Details* tab, scroll down to Camera.

STEPS for Aperture Priority Assignment

1. **Document how to access your camera's Aperture Priority settings:**

2. **Document how to Manually Focus your Lens:**

3. Place three **cans** side by side. Move the left can backward and right can forward.
4. Place each **card** against a can.
5. Place camera on a **tripod** and zoom all the way out (wide angle).
6. Open up to the widest aperture.
7. **Manually** focus on the center card.
8. What is your **focal length**? _____
9. What is your **f value**? _____
10. Zoom your lens in to get a closer shot of the three cards.
11. Open up to the widest aperture again.
12. **Manually** focus on the center card.
13. What is your **focal length**? _____
14. What is its **new f value**? _____
15. Do not change your focal length nor refocus for the rest of this assignment.
16. Starting with the **widest aperture** (answer from question 14) and stepping down to the **smallest aperture** (largest f number) snap a photo of the cards at each aperture step, half step, or third step.
17. Print, Cut, and Paste the widest aperture in the top box and the smallest aperture in the bottom box on the next page.
18. Document your findings, of both images, below that image.
19. Document the **File name**, **F number**, **Exposure time**, **ISO**, and **Focal Length**, of each image.
20. **Highlight** the Full Stops on the Image Information page using a marker.
21. **Overview**: Explain in your own words what is happening based on the image information data (and photos) plus draw a diagram showing aperture numbers vs. sizes. Make sure to underline key words and concepts.

WIDEST AND SMALLEST APERTURES

IMAGE INFORMATION

File name	F-Number	Exposure Time (Shutter Speed)	ISO	Focal Length

You may not need all the squares listed.

OVERVIEW

[Write your overview below. Draw a diagram of aperture sizes. Hint, remember the 1st floor and the basement.]

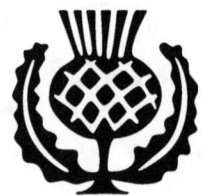

SHUTTER SPEED

The **shutter speed** determines how long the shutter is open. Usually when an image is snapped you will hear the clicking noise of the shutter. The shutter is like a curtain that opens and closes to let light enter your camera.

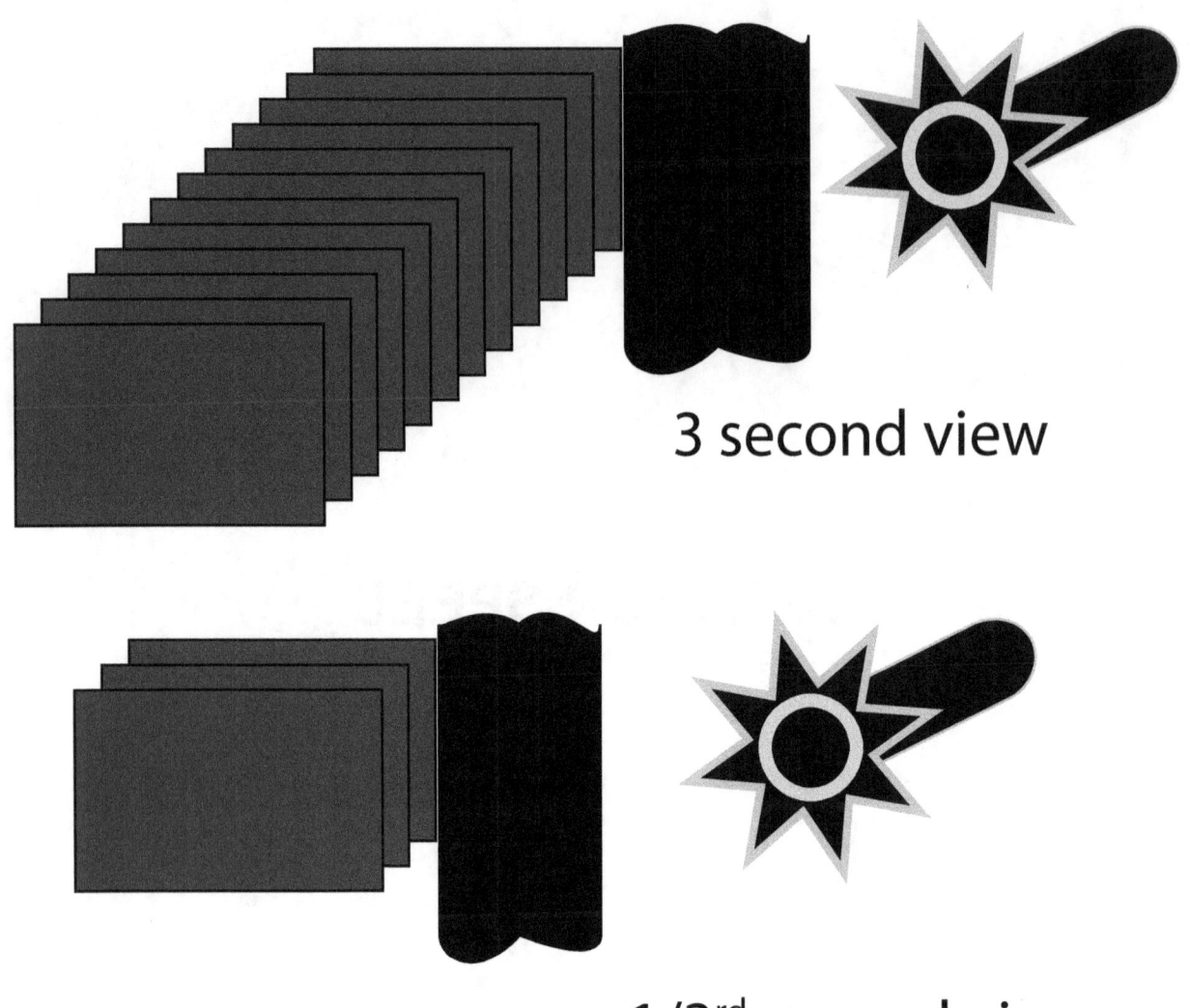

Shutter Speed Curtain

Imagine you have a flood light shining on a curtain. Behind the curtain is stacks of paper moving quickly from left to right. If the curtain is opened for 3 seconds the audience has enough time to see many sheets of paper. The audience also gets three seconds of light shinning on the paper which is a long time in photography terms. If the curtain, on the other hand, is opened for only 1/3rd second, the audience only has enough time to see a few sheets of paper then the curtain is closed again. Likewise, light is only shined on the paper for 1/3rd of a second. The above analogy is how a shutter works in a camera. The longer the shutter is opened then the more movement the camera captures. The shorter the shutter is opened, the less movement the camera captures.

Visualize **windshield wipers** on a car when it is raining. When the wipers are moving slowly your vision is blurred by water remaining on the glass.

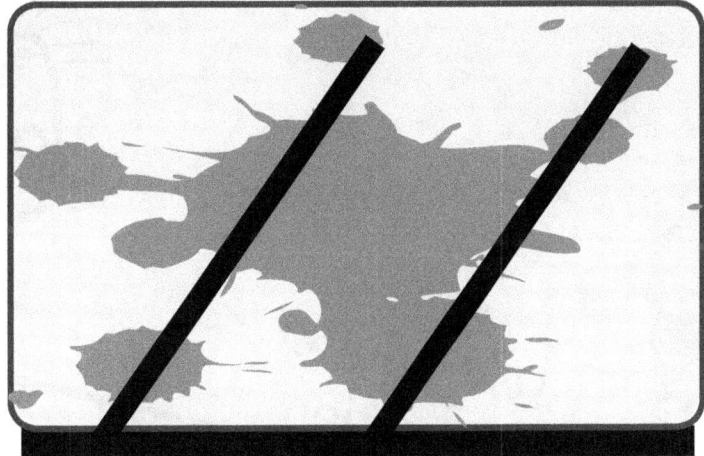
Windshield wipers moving slowly and blurred

When the wipers are going extremely fast then the glass remains clear.

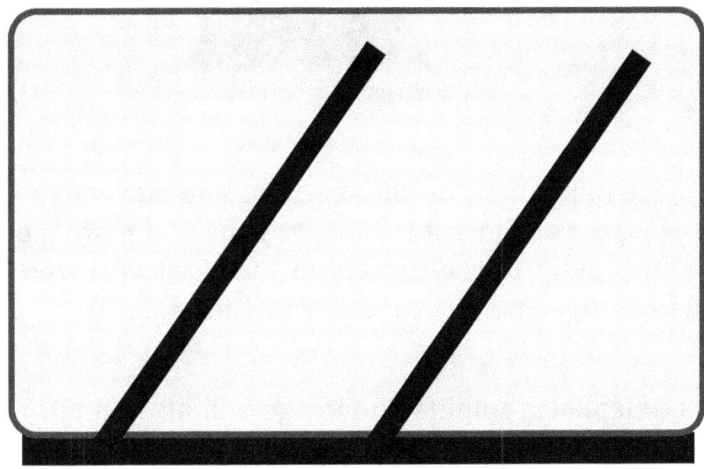
Windshield wipers moving fast and clear

The windshield wiper is like a shutter. Move it slowly, everything blurs. Move it quickly and everything is clear.

When determining shutter speed one should ask the question, "Is anything moving?" If yes then, "how do you want to capture the movement?" The longer the shutter is open then the more movement the camera can capture. The shorter the shutter is open then the less movement the camera can capture.

Therefore, if you want to:
    A.   **Freeze** the movement so it looks still, then use a **FAST** shutter speed.
    B.   **Blur** the movement to give a sense of motion, then use a **SLOW** shutter speed.

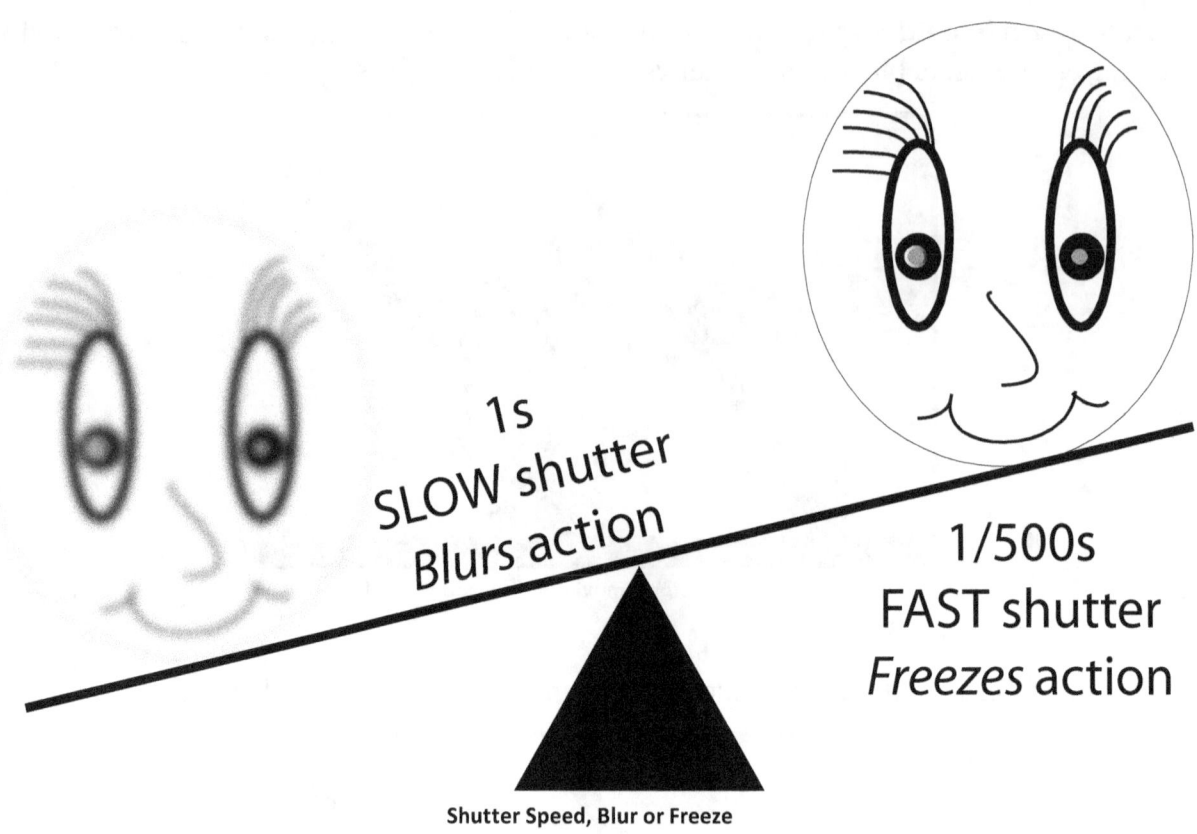

Shutter Speed, Blur or Freeze

Note the two smiley face individuals on the see-saw. The movement of the left person is blurred because the shutter is opened for a longer time and more movement is captured by the camera. The movement of the person on the right is frozen because we used a faster shutter speed (less movement is captured by the camera).

Longer focal lengths (telephoto) amplify the image and also amplify camera shake thus usually requiring a faster shutter speed. As a general rule, make sure the bottom number of the shutter speed is larger than the focal length of the lens. If, for example, the lens is 100mm, then 1/125th of a second shutter speed is a good starting place (125 is larger than 100).

Shutter speeds are measured in fractions of a second. The larger the denominator (bottom number) the faster the shutter opens and closes. For example, 1/1000 is much faster than 1/60. On most cameras, shutter speeds are as slow as 1 second and as fast as 1/1000th of a second.

Most of the time you will use a shutter speed of 1/60th of a second because anything slower is hard to use without a tripod. Any shutter speed slower than 1/60th a second should be used with a tripod.

Shutter speeds usually double in speed at each setting. For example 1/30, 1/60, 1/125 (125 is close to 120), 1/250, and so on.

Increasing a speed from 1/125 to 1/250 halves the light entering the camera. Decreasing a speed from 1/250 to 1/125 doubles the light entering the camera.

Outcome	Light	Shutter Speed	Denominator	Decimal	Seconds
Blur movement	More light	Slower	Smaller bottom #	1	1
↕	↕	↕	↕	.5	½
				.25	¼
				.125	1/8
				.067	1/15
				.033	1/30
				.017	1/60
				.008	1/125
				.004	1/250
				.002	1/500
Freeze movement	Less light	Faster	Larger bottom #	.001	1/1000

Shutter Speed

As on can see, increasing the shutter speed decreases the light entering the camera, and decreasing the shutter speed increases the light entering the camera. As a result, the shutter speeds you desire to use may change depending on whether you are indoors or outdoors.

If we begin with a 1 second shutter speed, then iterate through the shutter speeds by one stop, snapping an image at each iteration, until reaching 1/1000, then will obtain the following results for the different scenarios.

Scenario	Beginning Images	Ending Images
Indoors	OK	Underexposed (black - too dark)
Outdoors	Overexposed (white - too light)	OK
Shutter Speed	Slow (more light enters)	Fast (less light enters)
Aperture	Shallow Aperture (big f number)	Large Aperture (small f number)

Shutter Speed Scenario

Watch out!

Below are the possible scenarios of shutter speed lingo. Each scenario can possibly be on opposite ends of the chart.

Increase the shutter can mean:
Increase the TIME the shutter stays open (Slower Shutter Speeds).
Increase the SPEED in which the shutter opens and closes (Faster Shutter Speeds).
Decrease the TIME the shutter stays open (Faster Shutter Speeds).

Decrease the shutter can mean:
Decrease the TIME the shutter stays open (Faster Shutter Speeds).
Decrease the SPEED in which the shutter opens and closes (Slower Shutter Speeds).
Increase the TIME the shutter stays open (Slower Shutter Speeds).

Shutter Speed, from slow to fast chart

This book will normally refer to SPEED as opposed to TIME when referring to shutter speeds. Thus if a shutter speed is said to increase then it means the shutter opens and closes faster. If the shutter speed is said to decrease then it means the shutter opens and closes slower. Hence, a shutter speed increase is a faster shutter speed (from 1/500 to 1/1000); a shutter speed decrease is a slower shutter speed. The main thing is to know what shutter speed lingo a person is speaking in.

Shutter Speed, from fast to slow chart

The charts on this page move in both directions for the reader's convenience.

SHUTTER PRIORITY MODE

Most cameras contain a shutter priority mode. When a camera is in shutter priority mode, the user sets the shutter speed value and the camera automatically sets the correct aperture value.

Shutter Speed Priority is the **S** in our acronym MAP**S**.

It may be difficult understanding the nomenclature of your camera when trying to read the shutter speed values. The Control Panel (on the top of the camera) might display a number totally different than the LCD (on the back of the camera). Below is a table explaining how to read your camera's display. This information might change between camera manufactures so please consult your user guide.

Control Panel Display	LCD	Description
2"	2"	2 seconds
1.6"	1.6"	1.6 seconds
1.3"	1.3"	1.3 seconds
1	1	1 second
1.3	1/1.3	1/1.3 second
1.6	1/1.6	1/1.6 second
2.5	1/2.5	1/2.5 second
2	½	½ second
3	1/3	1/3rd second
4	¼	¼ second
8o	1/80	1/80 second
32o	1/32o	1/320 second
1ooo	1/1ooo	1/1000 second

Shutter Speed Decipher

Note how the ["] indicates a whole number such that the quotation mark distinguishes 5" from 5; where the former is 5 seconds and the later is 1/5 seconds. Also the lowercase letter O is used for fractions of time such that 1/500 seconds is written as 5oo.

Other considerations is whether the lens is in auto focus mode or manual mode. In many cases you will not get the desired results trying to use auto focus when working in aperture priority mode. As a result, the assignments require manually focusing the camera lens.

SHUTTER PRIORITY IN ACTION #1

Tools needed:
    Ceiling fan
    Camera
    Tripod
    User guide

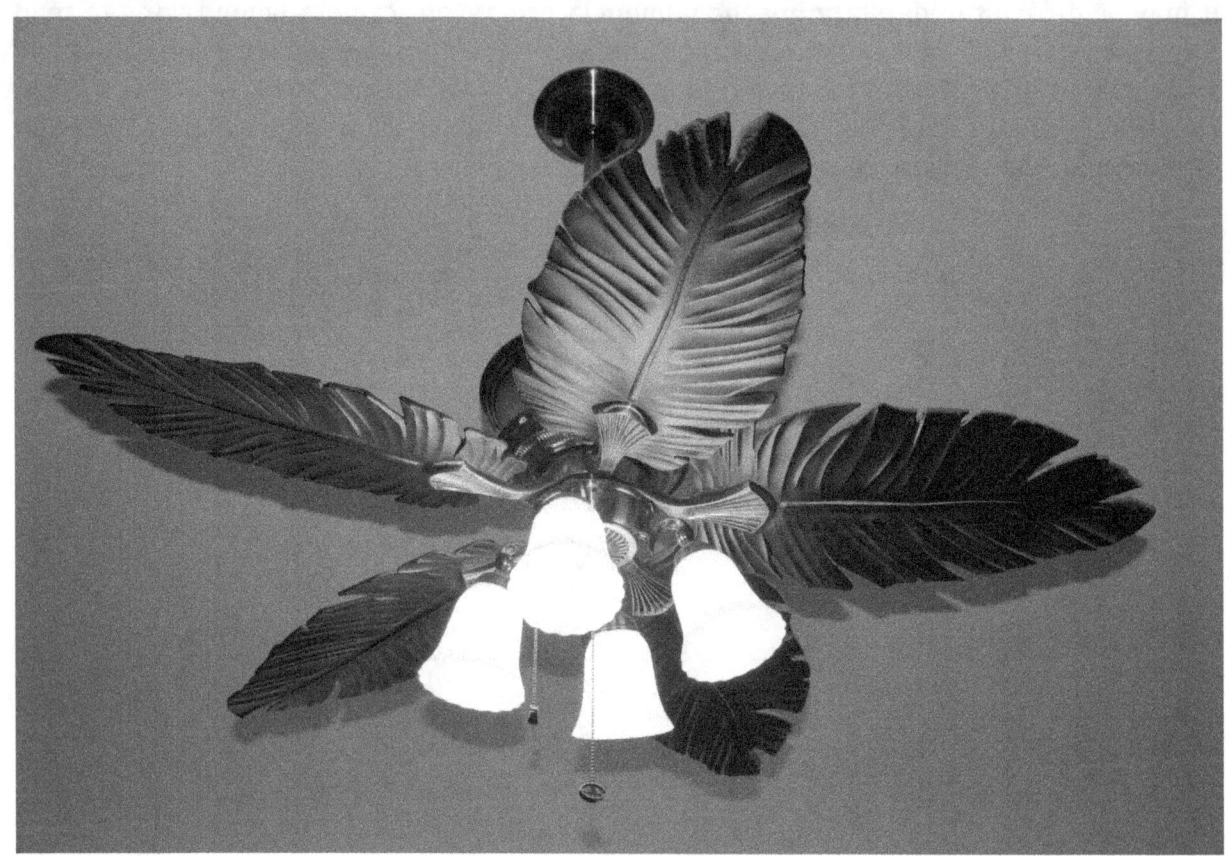

Shutter Speed, ceiling fan needed

This assignment will require accessing image information. To access the F number, Exposure time, ISO, and Focal Length, do the following:

- **MAC**: right click the file, select *Get Info*, then click the down arrow under *More Info*. You will need your camera's software to see the ISO settings on a MAC.
- **PC**: right click the file, select *Properties*, click the *Details* tab, scroll down to Camera.

Things to Note
Increasing the shutter speed decreases the light entering the camera. This can cause images to be too dark, a concept known as **underexposed**. Generally when we increase the shutter speed we also increase the **ISO** (to be covered later) to compensate for the decreased light entering the camera. Because we are focusing on ONE area of the camera at a time we will not adjust the ISO just yet. Therefore the ceiling fan project is to be done in a well lit area.

STEPS for Shutter Priority in Action #1

1. **Document how to access your camera's Shutter Speed Priority settings:**

On the Nikon D7100: Turn on the camera. Press the Mode dial lock release then turn the Mode dial to S aligning the S up with the white dot. Rotate the Main Command dial on the back of the camera to the left to make the shutter speed slower. Rotate the dial to the right to make the shutter speed faster. This camera's shutter speed goes from 30 seconds (slow) to 1/8000th of a second (fast). If the shutter speed values disappear before you make a selection, then press the Metering button at the top right of the camera (the Metering button has five dots on it).

2. **Document how to Manually Focus your Lens:**

On the Nikon D7100: The Focus-Mode selector, on the front of the camera, has the letters AF and M. Move the Focus-Mode selector to M. To manually focus the lens, adjust the lens's focusing ring until the image is clear.

3. What is your camera's slowest shutter speed? *30s*
4. What is your camera's fastest shutter speed? *1/8000*
5. Place camera on a **tripod** and zoom to get all blades of the fan in the image.
6. Turn the fan on **slow** speed.
7. **Manually** focus the lens as best as possible.
8. Do not refocus lens for the steps below.
9. Starting with the following shutter speeds (listed in seconds from slowest to fastest) snap a photo using each speed: 1, ½, ¼, 1/8, 1/15, 1/30, 1/60, 1/125, 1/250, 1/500, 1/1000.
10. Print, Cut, and Paste your image from the **1s** shutter speed in the top box and your image from the **1/15s** shutter speed in the bottom box.
11. Document your findings, of both images, below each image.
12. List the **File name, F number, Exposure time (shutter speed), ISO,** and **Focal Length**, of each image.
13. **Highlight** the 1s and 1/15s rows on the Image Information page using a marker.
14. **Overview**: Explain in your own words what is happening with the image information. Draw the relationship between shutter speed, light, and aperture size.

SHUTTER SPEEDS 1S AND 1/15S

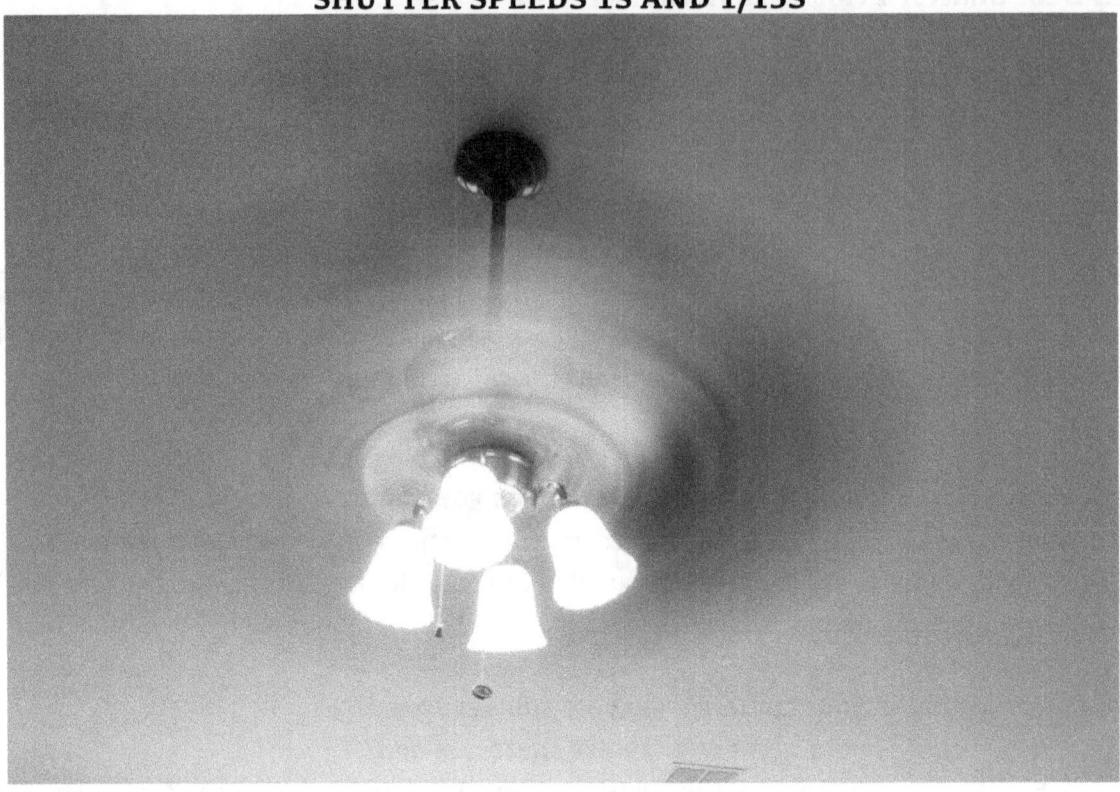

Shutter Speed at 1 second with ceiling fan

1 Second: The fan blades are blurred because the shutter is opened for a longer time and more movement is captured by the camera. Since the shutter is opened longer more light hits the sensor causing a lighter image.

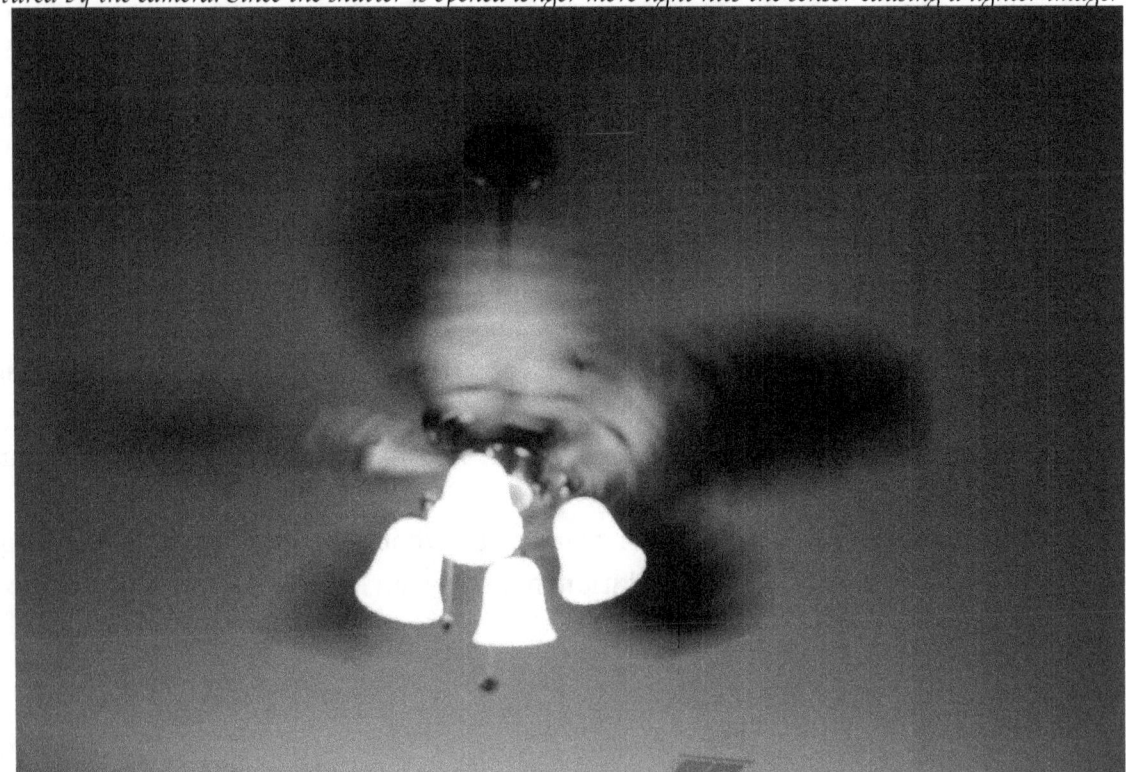

Shutter Speed at 1/15s with ceiling fan

1/15 Second: The fan blades are less blurred because the shutter opens and closes quickly, hence less movement is captured by the camera. A quick shutter means less light is hitting the sensor hence yielding darker images.

IMAGE INFORMATION

File name	F-Number	Exposure Time (Shutter Speed)	ISO	Focal Length
DSC_300.jpg	f11	1s	100	26mm
DSC_301.jpg	f8	1/2s	100	26mm
DSC_302.jpg	f5.6	1/4s	100	26mm
DSC_303.jpg	f4.5	1/8s	100	26mm
DSC_304.jpg	f3.8	1/15s	100	26mm
DSC_305.jpg	f3.8	1/30s	100	26mm
DSC_306.jpg	f3.8	1/60s	100	26mm
DSC_307.jpg	f3.8	1/125s	100	26mm
DSC_308.jpg	f3.8	1/250s	100	26mm
DSC_309.jpg	f3.8	1/500s	100	26mm
DSC_310.jpg	f3.8	1/1000s	100	26mm

Note how when the images are taken indoors there is not enough light hence we use images taken at 1s and 1/15s. Any image taken at a faster speed than 1/15s (like 1/30s, 1/60s, 1/125s, ...) is too dark and considered **underexposed**.

OVERVIEW

Reference image taken at 1 second and after:
At decreased <u>shutter speeds</u> (shutter opens and closes slowly) the shutter is staying open for a longer amount of time thus a larger amount of light is entering the camera and more movement is captured. When we capture more movement we get a <u>blurring effect</u>. Since the shutter is staying open longer (letting in more light) the width of the <u>aperture decreases</u> (larger f number) to compensate for the extra light. The ISO and Focal Length remain constant.

Reference image taken at 1/1000 second and before:
As the <u>shutter speed increases</u> (shutter opens and closes faster) it means the shutter is staying open a shorter amount of time thus a smaller amount of light is entering the camera and less movement is captured. When we capture less movement we get the <u>still effect</u>. Since the shutter is staying open shorter (letting in less light) the width of the <u>aperture increases</u> (smaller f number) to compensate for the less light. The ISO and Focal Length remain constant.

At 1/30s the fan blades are noticeably still (less movement) yet the image is too dark because the shutter is faster (larger bottom number) and less light is entering the camera. At 1/60s the image is mostly dark except around the lights. At 1/500s and 1/1000s all that can be seen are the lights – everything else is black. If the lights on the ceiling fan had not been on then at 1/125s and faster speeds we would have a completely black image. On my shots, the images are acceptable to about 1/15 seconds. Thereafter the images become too dark to be used.

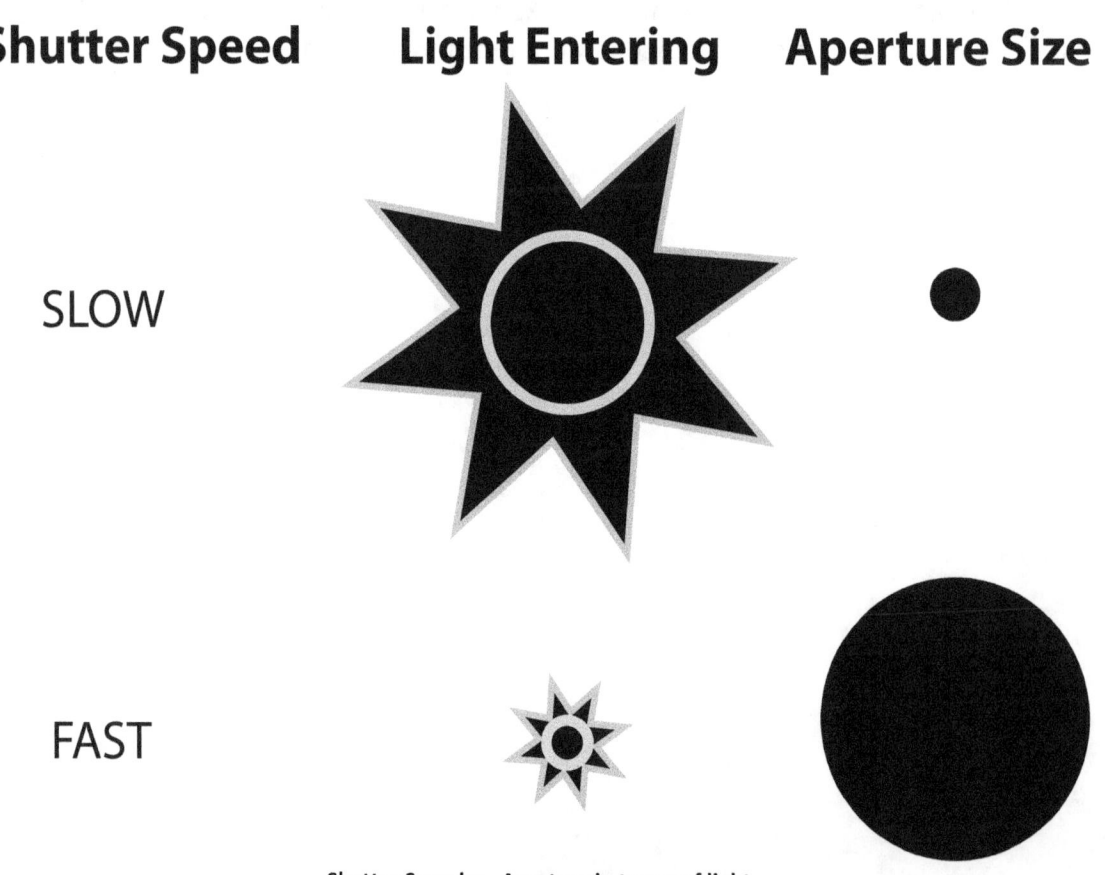

Shutter Speed vs. Aperture in terms of light

SHUTTER PRIORITY ASSIGNMENT #1

Tools needed:
    Fan (or optional ceiling fan)
    Yellow highlighter
    Camera
    Tripod
    User guide

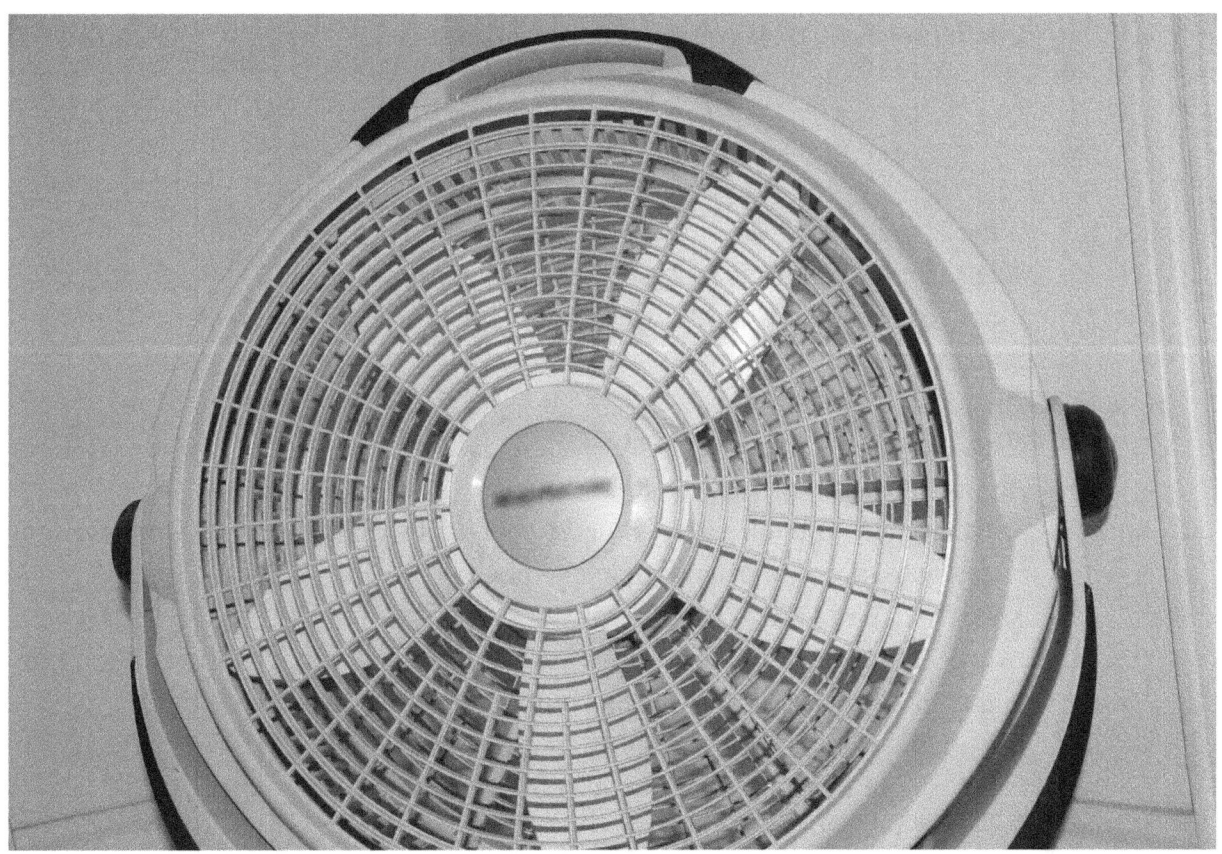

Shutter Priority fan

This assignment will require accessing image information. To access the F number, Exposure time, ISO, and Focal Length, do the following:

- **MAC**: right click the file, select *Get Info*, then click the down arrow under *More Info*. You will need your camera's software to see the ISO settings on a MAC.
- **PC**: right click the file, select *Properties*, click the *Details* tab, scroll down to Camera.

Things to Note
Increasing the shutter speed decreases the light entering the camera. This can cause your images to be too dark, a concept known as **underexposed**. Generally when we increase the shutter speed we also increase the **ISO** (to be covered later) to compensate for the decreased light entering the camera. Because we are focusing on ONE area of the camera at a time we will not adjust the ISO just yet. Therefore the fan project is to be done in a well lit area.

STEPS for Shutter Priority Assignment #1

1. **Document how to access your camera's Shutter Priority Speed settings:**

2. **Document how to Manually Focus your Lens:**

3. What is your camera's slowest shutter speed? _____
4. What is your camera's fastest shutter speed? _____
5. Place camera on a **tripod** and zoom to get all blades of the fan in the image.
6. Turn the fan on **slow** speed.
7. **Manually** focus the lens.
8. Do not refocus lens for the steps below.
9. Starting with the following shutter speeds (listed in seconds from slowest to fastest) snap a photo using each speed: 1, ½, ¼, 1/8, 1/15, 1/30, 1/60, 1/125, 1/250, 1/500, 1/1000.
10. Print, Cut, and Paste your image from the **1s** shutter speed in the top box and your image from the **1/15s** shutter speed in the bottom box.
11. Document your findings, of both images, below each image.
12. List the **File name**, **F number**, **Exposure time (shutter speed)**, **ISO**, and **Focal Length**, of each image.
13. **Highlight** the 1s and 1/15s rows on the Image Information page using a marker.
14. **Overview**: Explain in your own words what is happening with the image information. Draw a diagram of how shutter speed works.

SHUTTER SPEEDS 1S AND 1/15S

IMAGE INFORMATION

File name	F-Number	Exposure Time (Shutter Speed)	ISO	Focal Length
		1s		
		1/2s		
		1/4s		
		1/8s		
		1/15s		
		1/30s		
		1/60s		
		1/125s		
		1/250s		
		1/500s		
		1/1000s		

OVERVIEW

[Write your overview below. Draw a diagram of how shutter speeds work. Hint, remember the see-saw or windshield wipers.]

SHUTTER PRIORITY IN ACTION #2

Tools needed:
    Outdoor water flow
    Yellow highlighter
    Camera
    Tripod
    User guide

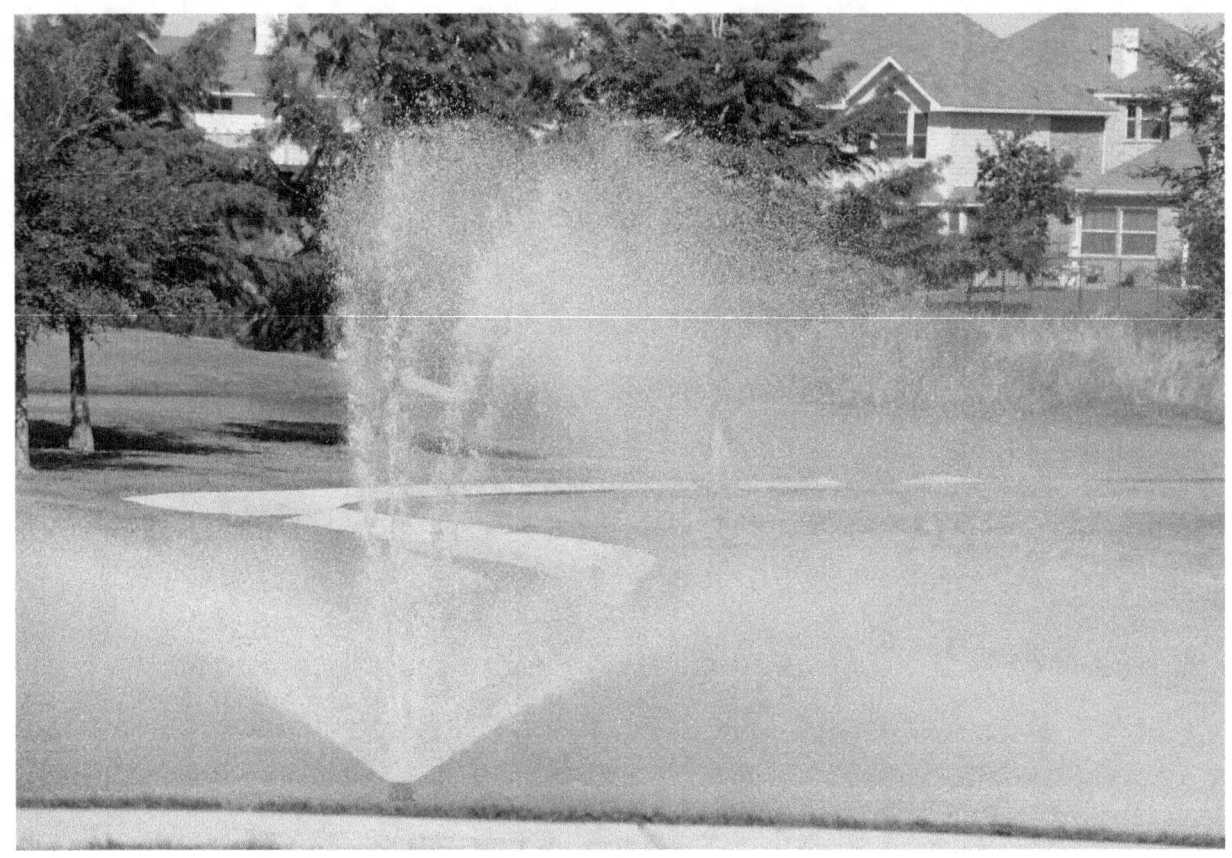

Shutter Speed water source

This assignment will require accessing image information. To access the F number, Exposure time, ISO, and Focal Length, do the following:

- **MAC**: right click the file, select *Get Info*, then click the down arrow under *More Info*. You will need your camera's software to see the ISO settings on a MAC.
- **PC**: right click the file, select *Properties*, click the *Details* tab, scroll down to Camera.

Things to Note

Slowing the shutter speed (keeping the shutter opened longer) increases the light entering the camera. This can cause your images to be too light, a concept known as **overexposed**. Generally when we decrease (keep shutter opened longer) the shutter speed we also decrease the **ISO** (to be covered later) to compensate for the increased light entering the camera, and we adjust the **exposure compensation** (to be covered later). Because we are focusing on ONE area of the camera at a time we will not adjust the ISO nor the Exposure compensation just yet.

STEPS for Shutter Priority in Action #2

1. **Document how to access your camera's shutter speed settings:**

On the Nikon D7100: Turn on the camera. Press the Mode dial lock release then turn the <u>Mode dial to S</u> aligning the S up with the white dot. Rotate the <u>Main Command</u> dial on the back of the camera to the left to make the shutter speed slower. Rotate the dial to the right to make the shutter speed faster. This camera's shutter speed goes from 30 seconds (slow) to $1/8000^{th}$ of a second (fast). If the shutter speed values disappear before you make a selection, then press the Metering button at the top right of the camera (the Metering button has five dots on it).

2. **Document how to Manually Focus your Lens:**

On the Nikon D7100: The Focus-Mode selector, on the front of the camera, has the letters AF and M. Move the Focus-Mode selector to M. To manually focus the lens, adjust the lens's focusing ring until the image is clear.

3. What is your camera's slowest shutter speed? *30s*
4. What is your camera's fastest shutter speed? *1/8000*
5. Place camera on a **tripod** and zoom to get a good view of the water in the image.
6. **Manually** focus the lens.
7. Do not refocus lens for the steps below.
8. Starting with the following shutter speeds (listed in seconds from slowest to fastest) snap a photo using each speed: 1, ½, ¼, 1/8, 1/15, 1/30, 1/60, 1/125, 1/250, 1/500, 1/1000.
9. Print, Cut, and Paste your image from the **1/15s** shutter speed in the top box and your image from the **1/1000s** shutter speed in the bottom box.
10. Document your findings, of both images, below that image.
11. List the **File name**, **F number**, **Exposure time (shutter speed)**, **ISO**, and **Focal Length**, of each image.
12. **Highlight** the 1s and 1/15s rows on the Image Information page using a marker.
13. **Overview**: Explain in your own words what is happening with the image information. Draw a diagram of anything that works like a shutter.

SHUTTER SPEEDS 1/15sS AND 1/1000S

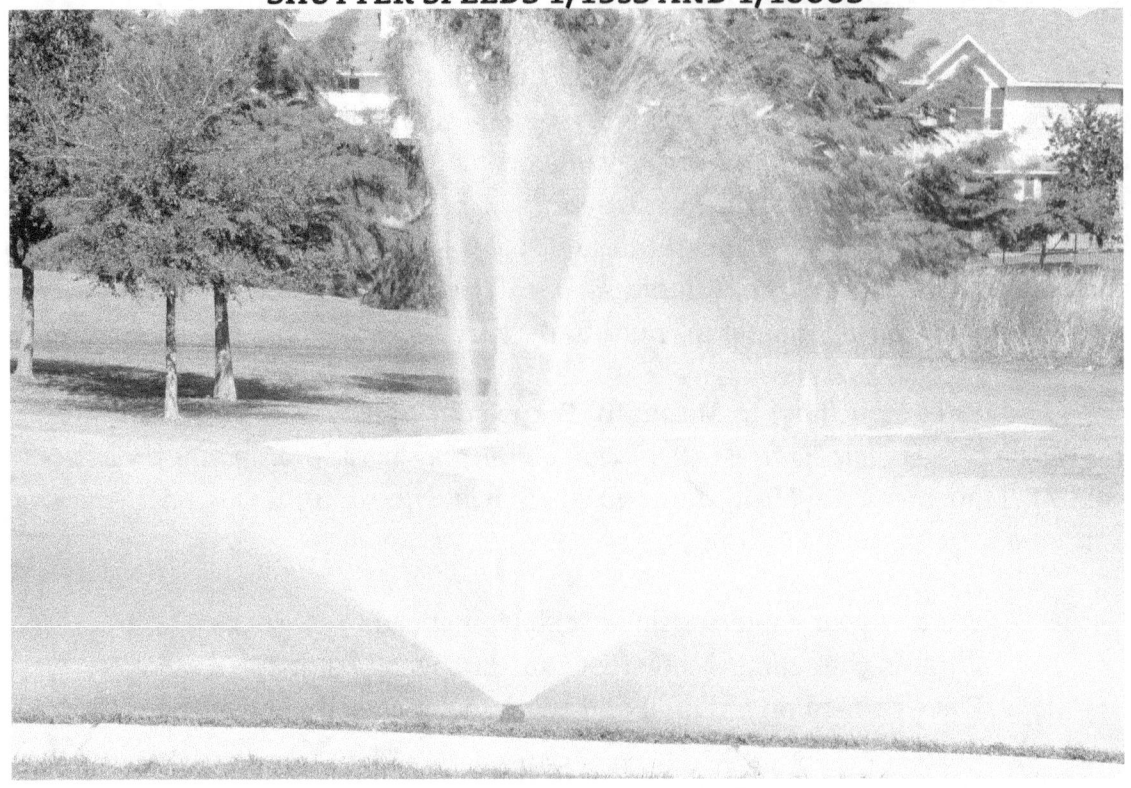

Shutter Speed outdoor water source 1/15s

1/15 Second: The water is blurred because the shutter is opened for a longer time and more movement is captured by the camera. Since the shutter is opened longer more light hits the sensor.

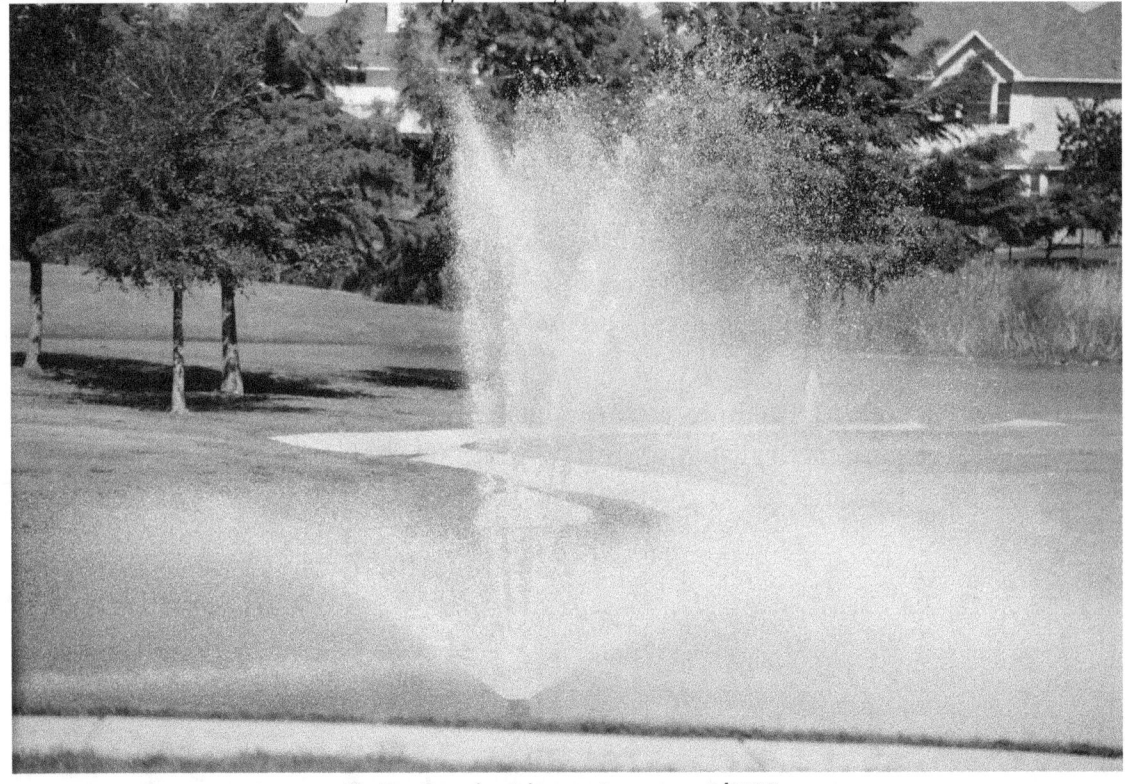

Shutter Speed outdoor water source 1/1000s

1/1000 Second: The water is less blurred because the shutter is opened for a shorter time hence less movement is captured by the camera. A quick shutter means less light hits the sensor hence the image is darker.

IMAGE INFORMATION

File name	F-Number	Exposure Time (Shutter Speed)	ISO	Focal Length
DSC_350.jpg	f25	1s	100	155mm
DSC_351.jpg	f25	1/2s	100	155mm
DSC_352.jpg	f25	1/4s	100	155mm
DSC_353.jpg	f25	1/8s	100	155mm
DSC_354.jpg	f25	1/15s	100	155mm
DSC_355.jpg	f25	1/30s	100	155mm
DSC_356.jpg	f18	1/60s	100	155mm
DSC_357.jpg	f14	1/125s	100	155mm
DSC_358.jpg	f10	1/250s	100	155mm
DSC_359.jpg	f7.1	1/500s	100	155mm
DSC_360.jpg	f5	1/1000s	100	155mm

Note how when images are taken outdoors there is a lot of light hence we used images taken at 1/15s and 1/1000s. Any image taken at a slower speed than 1/15s (like 1s, 1/2s, 1/4s, and 1/8s) is too bright and is considered **overexposed**.

OVERVIEW

As the shutter speed decreases (shutter opens and closes slower) it means the shutter is staying open for a longer amount of time thus a larger amount of light is entering the camera and more movement is captured. The extra light entering the camera can be seen at the slower shutter speeds from 1/2 second to 1/8 second as the corresponding images are extremely overexposed. The 1 second image is almost completely white. When we capture more movement we get a blurring effect. At 1/15s the water has a haze look. It is softer and less defined. Since the shutter is staying open longer (letting in more light) the width of the aperture decreases (larger f number, f25) to compensate for the extra light. The ISO and Focal Length remain constant.

As the shutter speed increases (opens and closes faster) it means the shutter is staying open a shorter amount of time thus a smaller amount of light is entering the camera and less movement is captured. The decrease in light entering the camera can be seen at the faster shutter speeds like 1/500 and 1/1000. When we capture less movement we get the still effect. Since the shutter is staying open shorter (letting in less light) the width of the aperture increases (smaller f number, f5) to compensate for the less light. The ISO and Focal Length remain constant.

If the water assignment had been done indoors then we would have the opposite affect. That is, instead of the beginning images being overexposed (too light) and the latter images being OK, the beginning images would be OK, and the latter images would be underexposed (too dark). In other words, for this outdoor assignment the beginning image is almost totally white. If this same assignment was done indoors then the ending image would be almost totally black.

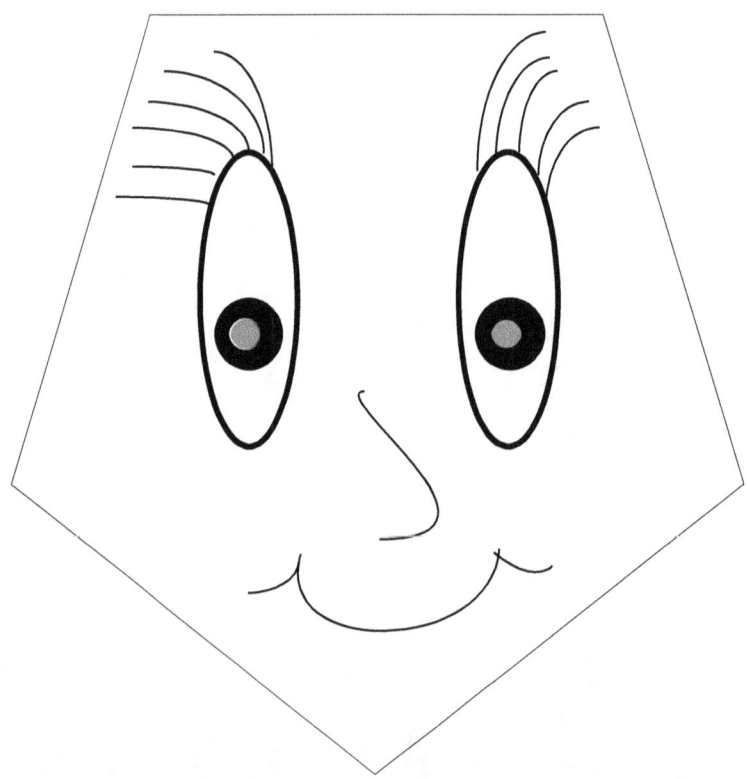

Eyes open and close like a shutter

SHUTTER PRIORITY ASSIGNMENT #2

Tools needed:
- Kitchen faucet (running water)
- Yellow highlighter
- Camera
- Tripod
- User guide

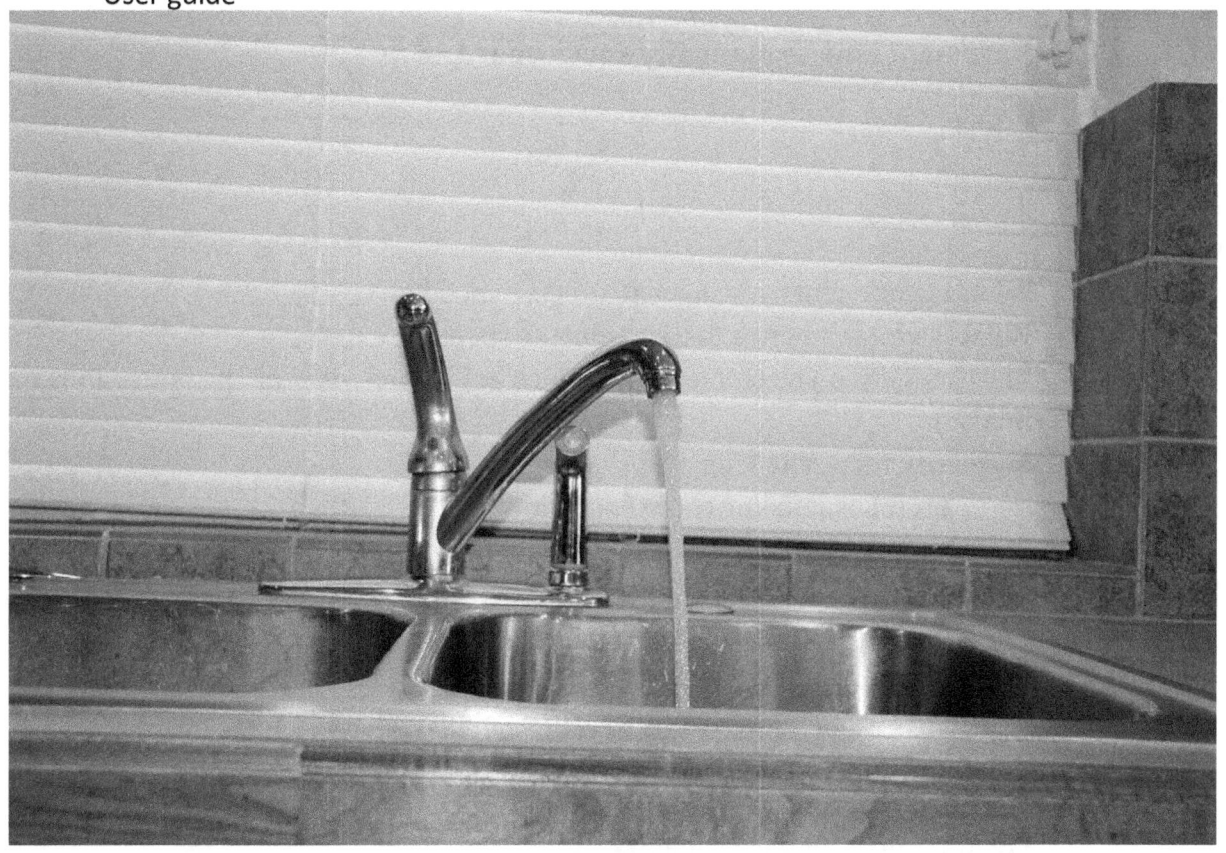

Shutter Speed indoor water source

This assignment will require accessing image information. To access the F number, Exposure time, ISO, and Focal Length, do the following:

- **MAC**: right click the file, select *Get Info*, then click the down arrow under *More Info*. You will need your camera's software to see the ISO settings on a MAC.
- **PC**: right click the file, select *Properties*, click the *Details* tab, scroll down to Camera.

Things to Note

Increasing the shutter speed decreases the light entering the camera. This can cause images to be too dark, a concept known as **underexposed**. Generally when we increase the shutter speed we also increase the **ISO** (to be covered later) to compensate for the decreased light entering the camera. Because we are focusing on ONE area of the camera at a time we will not adjust the ISO just yet. Therefore the water faucet project is to be done in a well lit area.

Be careful not to get moisture in your camera!

STEPS for Shutter Priority Assignment #2

1. **Document how to access your camera's shutter speed settings:**

2. **Document how to Manually Focus your Lens:**

3. What is your camera's slowest shutter speed? _____
4. What is your camera's fastest shutter speed? _____
5. Place camera on a **tripod** and zoom to get a good view of the water in the image.
6. **Manually** focus the lens.
7. Do not refocus lens for the steps below.
8. Starting with the following shutter speeds (listed in seconds from slowest to fastest) snap a photo using each speed: 1, ½, ¼, 1/8, 1/15, 1/30, 1/60, 1/125, 1/250, 1/500, 1/1000.
9. Print, Cut, and Paste your image from the **1/15s** shutter speed in the top box and your image from the **1/1000s** shutter speed in the bottom box.
10. Document your findings, of both images, below that image.
11. List the **File name**, **F number**, **Exposure time (shutter speed)**, **ISO**, and **Focal Length**, of each image.
12. **Highlight** the 1/15s and 1/1000s rows on the Image Information page.
13. **Overview**: Explain in your own words what is happening with the image information. Draw a diagram of how shutter speed works.

SHUTTER SPEEDS 1/15s AND 1/1000S

IMAGE INFORMATION

File name	F-Number	Exposure Time (Shutter Speed)	ISO	Focal Length
		1s		
		1/2s		
		1/4s		
		1/8s		
		1/15s		
		1/30s		
		1/60s		
		1/125s		
		1/250s		
		1/500s		
		1/1000s		

OVERVIEW

[Write your overview below. Draw a diagram of how shutter speeds work. Hint, remember the see-saw or windshield wipers.]

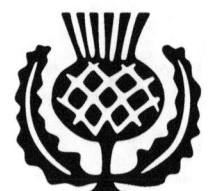

PROGRAM MODE

Program Mode is the **P** in our acronym MA**P**S.

In **automatic mode** your camera takes care of everything. Program mode is a flexible form of automatic mode which allows the photographer full control of certain camera aspects.

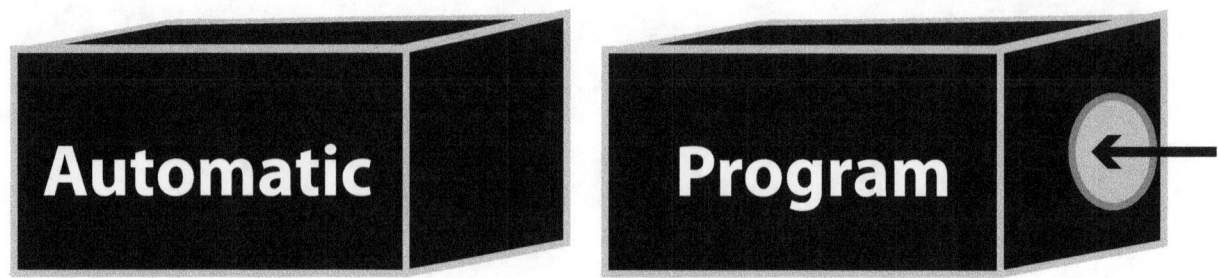
Automatic Box vs. Program Box

Visualize a closed box where the user has no access to what is inside the box. The closed box is symbolic of the camera's automatic mode. Now visualize a closed box with a small hole that the photographer can tap into to make some changes. The later is symbolic of the camera's program mode.

In Aperture Priority Mode the user selects the aperture and the camera selects the appropriate Shutter Speed. In Shutter Speed Priority Mode, the user selects the shutter speed and the camera selects the appropriate aperture. In Program Mode the user can select a different combination of aperture and shutter speed and the camera returns the correct **exposure** (to be covered later).

When a photographer normally shoots in full automatic mode yet wants to make a simple change, like adjusting **White Balance** (to be discussed later), and changing **ISO** (to be discussed later) then the Program mode is the recommended method.

Below is a table describing the functions selected by the photographer and the functions selected by the camera.

Mode	Shutter Speed selected by:	Aperture selected by
M (manual)	photographer	photographer
A (aperture priority)	camera	photographer
P (programmed)	camera	camera
S (shutter priority)	photographer	camera

Functions selected by Photographer and Camera

We will work with using Program Mode later.

PROGRAMMED MODE IN ACTION

Tools needed:
    Camera
    User guide

Document how to access your camera's Programmed Mode

On the Nikon D7100, press the <u>Mode dial lock release</u> button (top of camera) and rotate the mode dial to P. The P should be aligned to the white dot.

PROGRAMMED MODE ASSIGNMENT

Tools needed:
    Camera
    User guide

Document how to access <u>your</u> camera's Programmed Mode
[*Be sure to document the brand and model number of your camera*]

ISO SENSITIVITY

ISO determines how sensitive your camera's **eye** (imaging sensor) is to light. The term and concept of ISO is carried over from the days of film.

The lower the ISO number, the less sensitive the camera is to light, hence more light is needed to create a descent exposure (covered later). The higher the ISO number, the more sensitive the camera is to light, hence less light is needed to create a descent exposure.

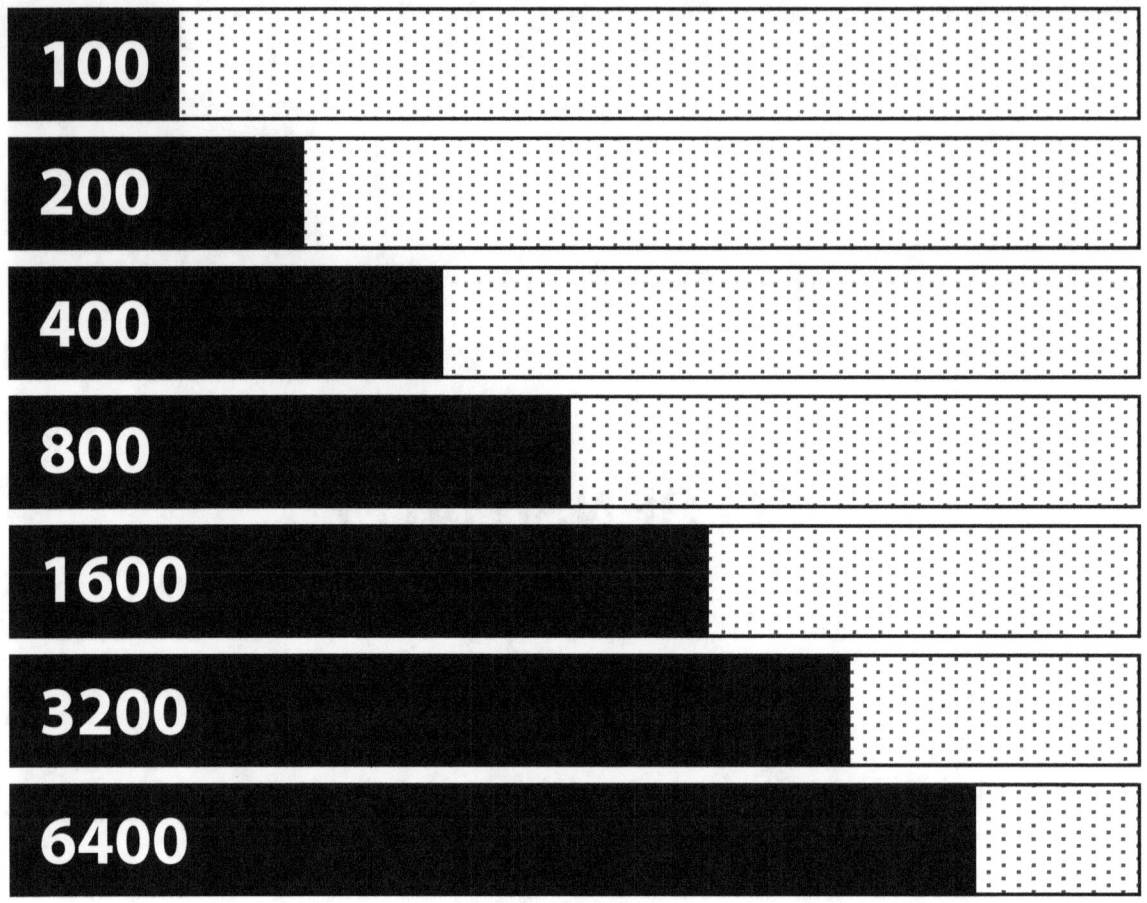

ISO Light graph

On the image above, the black rectangles on the left represent the ISO number. The dotted rectangles on the right represent the light needed with that corresponding ISO number. Note how when the ISO number is small then a lot of light is needed for a correct exposure, yet, as the ISO number increases, the amount of light needed for a correct exposure decreases.

Lower ISO numbers are great for outdoor shooting in bright daylight. The lower the ISO number then the less noise (grain) that will appear in your image.

Higher ISO numbers are great for indoor shooting with low light levels. The higher the ISO number then the more noise (grain) that will appear in your image.

ISO numbers on many point and shoot cameras range from 50 - 400. On mid-level dSLR cameras the ISO range might be from 100 – 6400.

Although keeping a camera at a high ISO number will guarantee that a photographer always has sufficient light, it is not wise to do so as higher ISO numbers produce more noise (grain look) in photographs than lower ISO numbers. The lower the ISO number the sharper and crisper the image.

If an ISO number changes from 100 to 200 then the ISO has doubled in sensitivity by one stop. If the ISO changes from 200 to 100 then the ISO has been halved in sensitivity by one stop. In the days of film, a low ISO number was considered a slow film and a high ISO number was considered a fast film.

ISO Behavior

Turtle or Rabbit	Detail	Light needed	Location	Film Speed (ISO)
Slow film	Greater detail	More light needed	Outdoors	100
↕	↕	↕	↕	200
				400
				800
				1600
				3200
Fast film	Less detail	Less light needed	Indoors	6400

ISO Behavior similar to Film Speed

Note how ISO 100 needs more light. This can be accomplished by one of the following:
1. Keep the shutter opened longer to allow in more light.
2. Open the aperture wider (smaller f number) to allow more light to enter.
3. Keep the shutter opened longer and open the aperture wider.

Note how ISO 6400 needs less light. This can be accomplished by one of the following:
1. Keep the shutter opened shorter to allow in less light.
2. Stop the aperture down (bigger f number) to allow less light to enter.
3. Keep the shutter opened shorter and stop the aperture down.

Any ISO number between ISO 100 and ISO 6400 follows the same principle respectively.

ISO SENSITIVITY IN ACTION

Tools needed:
    Low light location
    Camera
    Tripod
    User guide

ACCESSING IMAGE INFORMATION

This assignment will require accessing image information. To access the F number, Exposure time, ISO, and Focal Length, do the following:

- **MAC**: right click the file, select *Get Info*, then click the down arrow under *More Info*. You will need your camera's software to see the ISO settings on a MAC.
- **PC**: right click the file, select *Properties*, click the *Details* tab, scroll down to Camera.

Things to Note

Your images will look the same when viewed as small sizes. Once the image is magnified then the differences in texture will show.

STEPS for ISO in Action

1. **Document how to access your camera's ISO settings:**

   On the Nikon D7100: Turn on the camera. At the left back of the camera press the dual icon button (the magnifying glass icon next to the cross alignment icon, the words ISO are typed above the icons) then rotate the main command dial until the desired ISO number appears in the control panel or the viewfinder.

2. **Document how to Manually Focus your Lens:**

   On the Nikon D7100: Move the Focus-Mode selector to M. The Focus-Mode selector is on the front of the camera and has the letters AF and M stamped above it. To manually focus the lens, adjust the lens's focusing ring until the image is clear. The focusing ring is behind the zoom area of the lens.

3. **Document how to place your camera in Programmed Mode.**

   On the Nikon D7100, press the Mode dial lock release button (top of camera) and rotate the <u>Mode dial to P</u>. The P should be aligned to the white dot.

4. Place your camera in **Programmed Mode**.
5. Place camera on a **tripod**.
6. **Manually** focus on an item or area of your choice in extremely low light.
7. What is your camera's **lowest ISO** value? *ISO 100*
8. What is your camera's **highest ISO** value? *ISO 25600*
9. Do not change your focal length nor refocus for the rest of this assignment.
10. Starting with the **lowest ISO** and moving up to the **highest ISO** in **one stop** increments, snap a photo of your choice, but of the same thing. Do not snap images beyond ISO 6400.
11. Magnify the smallest ISO image and the largest ISO image. Look at the difference in quality at larger magnifications.
12. Print, Cut, and Paste the smallest ISO in the top box and the largest ISO in the bottom box on the next page.
13. Document your findings, of both images, below that image.
14. Document the **File name**, **F number**, **Exposure time**, **ISO**, and **Focal Length**, of each image.
15. View all of your ISO images **enlarged**. What is the highest ISO value where the images are still acceptable in quality. *ISO 800*
16. **Optional**: enlarge the smallest ISO image and the largest ISO image, crop out an equivalent area and past below your image information table. Document what you notice.
17. **Overview**: Explain in your own words what is happening based on the image information data (and photos). Make sure to underline key words and concepts. Explain what would have happened if the camera had been in Aperture Priority Mode. Explain what would have happened if the camera had been in Shutter Priority Mode. Add your final thoughts on the subject.

SMALLEST AND LARGEST ISO

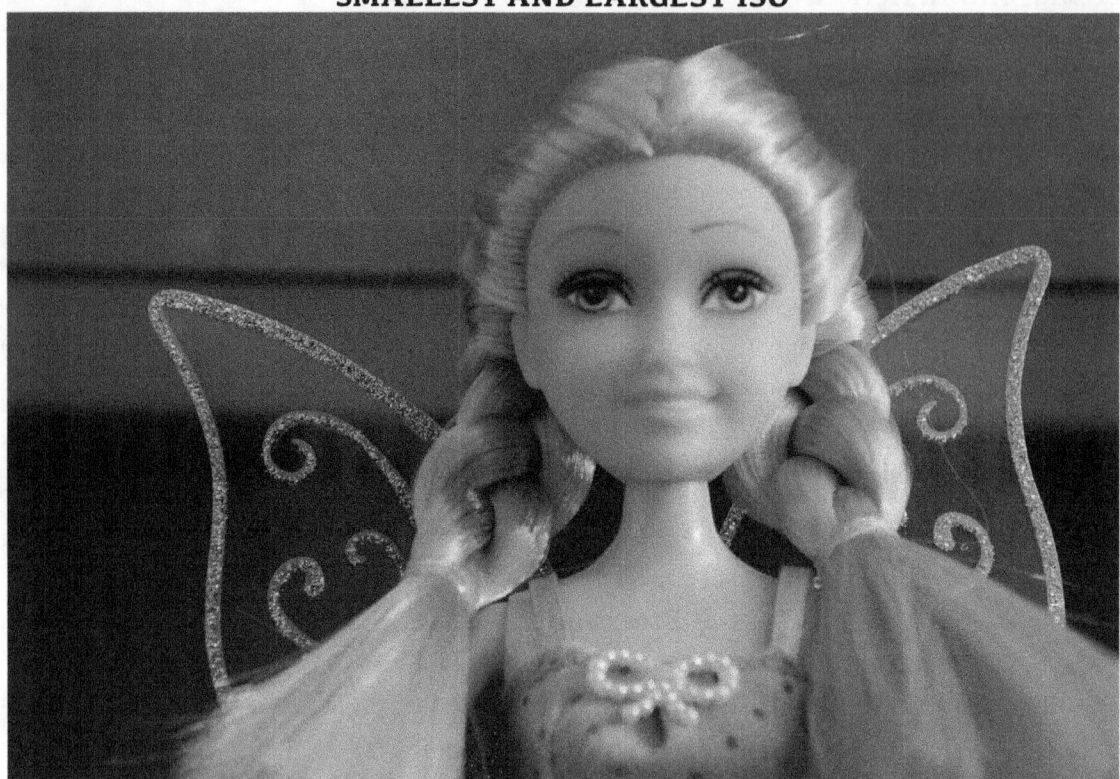

ISO 100 image

At ISO 100 the image looks fine. This is possibly because I am using the Nikon d7100 with a larger sensor which handles low light situations well.

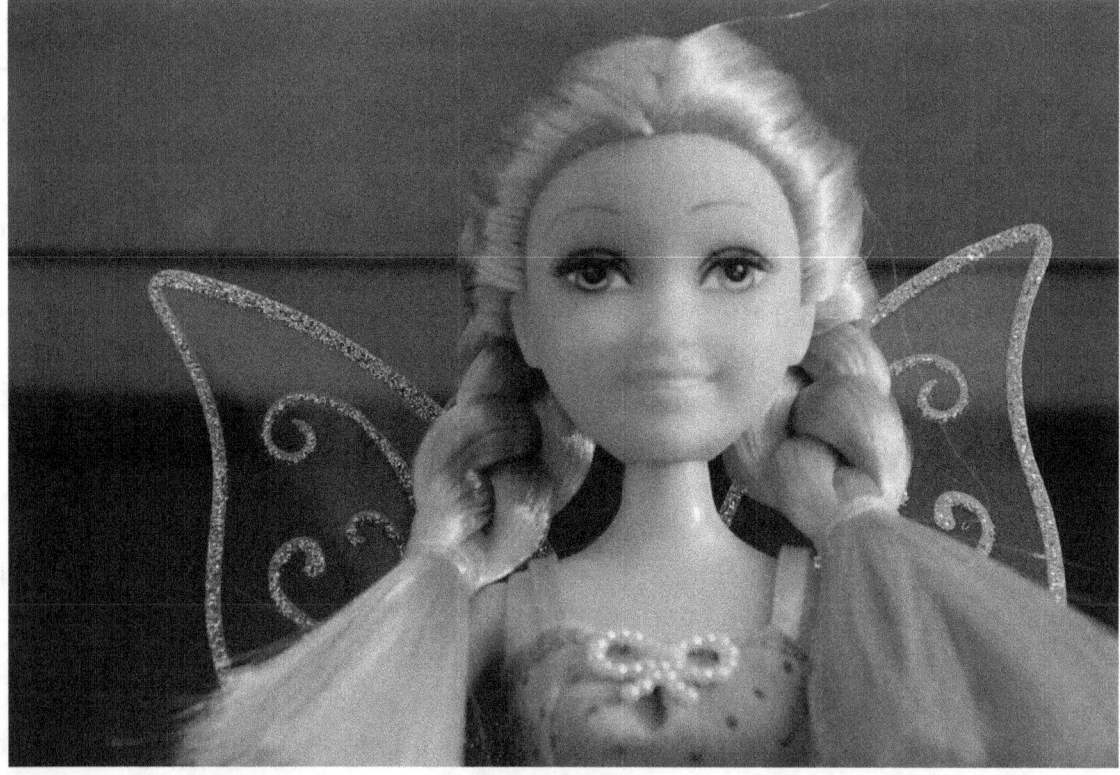

ISO 6400 image

At ISO 6400 the image looks the same (to the untrained eye) as the ISO 100 image at size 4x6. When the image is increased in size the noise shows and the difference between ISO 100 and ISO 6400 is apparent.

IMAGE INFORMATION

File name	F-Number	Exposure Time (Shutter Speed)	ISO	Focal Length
DSC_400.jpg	f8	13s	100	56mm
DSC_401.jpg	f8	6s	200	56mm
DSC_402.jpg	f8	3s	400	56mm
DSC_403.jpg	f8	1.6s	800	56mm
DSC_404.jpg	f8	1/1.3s	1600	56mm
DSC_405.jpg	f8	1/2.5s	3200	56mm
DSC_406.jpg	f8	1/5s	6400	56mm

ISO image information table

Optional step #16

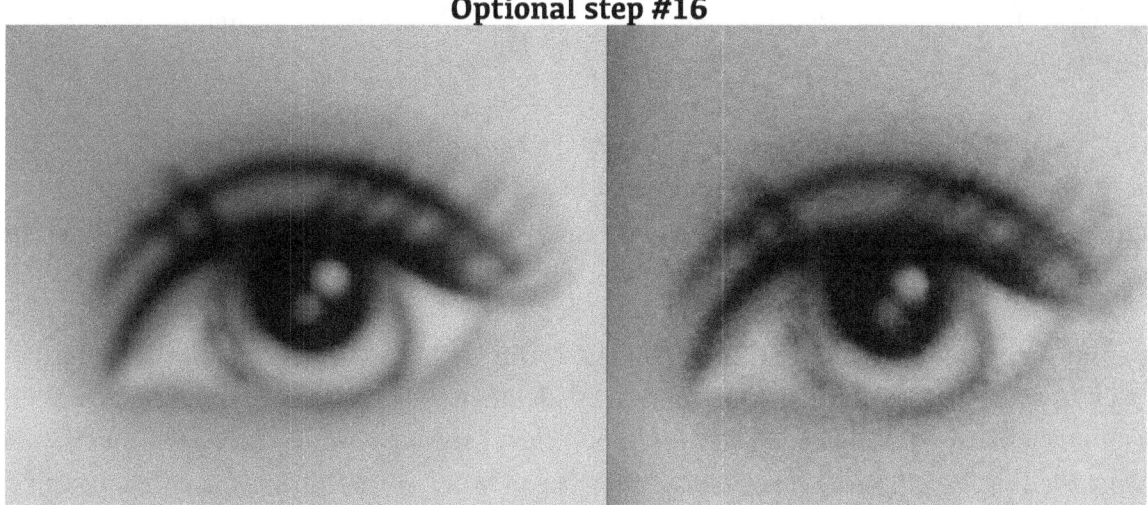

ISO Enlargement comparison

ISO 100 is the eye to the left. ISO 6400 is the eye to the right. Both images were enlarged to the same size. Note how there is more grain (noise) on the image to the right.

OVERVIEW

Throughout this imaging sequence the aperture remained at a constant f8. The shutter speed changed in response to ISO changes. At low ISO numbers, where more light is needed to create a correct exposure, the shutter remained opened for a longer period of time to allow more light to enter the camera. At higher ISO numbers, where less light is needed to make a descent exposure, the shutter remained opened for a shorter period of time to reduce the amount of light entering the camera.

The aperture being at f8 is a result of the selected focal length of 56mm. If the focal length had been 18mm then the aperture would be f3.5. I know this because I adjusted the focal length to 18mm and watched the aperture change to f3.5. As I spanned through one stop ISO increments the aperture remained constant at f3.5 based on the focal length. The aperture will not always remain constant. On another test where I shot images of a candle, with only the candle's light, the aperture remained constant at f4.2 until ISO 6400 in which the aperture changed to f5.

All images are basically indistinguishable to the untrained eye when viewed at sizes around 4x6. When the images are enlarged then more grain (noise) appears on the images shot at a higher ISO.

Based on the image information table, when the ISO is set to 100, if the camera is in Aperture Priority Mode (instead of Programmed Mode) then I will need an aperture value of f8 to obtain a decent exposure. If I decrease my aperture value two stops to f16 (f8, f11, f16) then the image will be underexposed and hence too dark.

Based on the image information table, when the ISO is set to 100, if the camera is in Shutter Speed Priority Mode (instead of Programmed Mode) then I will need a 13s shutter speed to obtain a decent exposure. If I use 1/5s at ISO 100 then the image will be too dark (underexposed) because the shutter will not be open long enough to allow for sufficient light to enter the camera.

My final thoughts: What I found surprising is that the f stop stayed constant. I had thought the aperture would be more opened at the lower ISO number to allow in more light (low ISO number, low f number). Instead, the shutter stayed opened longer to allow more light to enter.

ISO SENSITIVITY ASSIGNMENT

Tools needed:
    Any low light location (preferably an outdoor night shot)
    Camera
    Tripod
    User guide

ACCESSING IMAGE INFORMATION

This assignment will require accessing image information. To access the F number, Exposure time, ISO, and Focal Length, do the following:

- **MAC**: right click the file, select *Get Info*, then click the down arrow under *More Info*. You will need your camera's software to see the ISO settings on a MAC.
- **PC**: right click the file, select *Properties*, click the *Details* tab, scroll down to Camera.

Things to Note

Your images will look the same when viewed as small sizes. Once the image is magnified then the differences in texture will show.

STEPS for ISO Sensitivity Assignment

1. **Document how to access your camera's ISO settings:**

2. **Document how to Manually Focus your Lens:**

3. **Document how to place your camera in Programmed Mode.**

4. Place your camera in **Programmed Mode**.
5. Place camera on a **tripod**.
6. **Manually** focus on an item or area of your choice in extremely low light.
7. What is your camera's **lowest ISO** value? _____
8. What is your camera's **highest ISO** value? _____
9. Do not change your focal length nor refocus for the rest of this assignment.
10. Starting with the **lowest ISO** and moving up to the **highest ISO** in **one stop** increments, snap a photo of your choice, but of the same thing. Do not snap images beyond ISO 6400.
11. Magnify the smallest ISO image and the largest ISO image. Look at the difference in quality at larger magnifications.
12. Print, Cut, and Paste the smallest ISO in the top box and the largest ISO in the bottom box on the next page.
13. Document your findings, of both images, below that image.
14. Document the **File name**, **F number**, **Exposure time**, **ISO**, and **Focal Length**, of each image.
15. View all of your ISO images **enlarged**. Document the highest ISO where the images are still acceptable in quality. _____
16. **Optional**: enlarge the smallest ISO image and the largest ISO image, crop out an equivalent area and past below your image information table. Document what you notice.
17. **Overview**: Explain in your own words what is happening based on the image information data (and photos). Make sure to underline key words and concepts. Explain what would have happened if the camera had been in Aperture Priority Mode. Explain what would have happened if the camera had been in Shutter Priority Mode. Add your final thoughts on the subject.

SMALLEST AND LARGEST ISO

IMAGE INFORMATION

File name	F-Number	Exposure Time (Shutter Speed)	ISO	Focal Length

Optional step #16 below

OVERVIEW

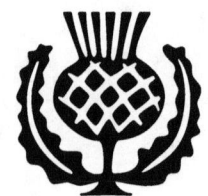

EXPOSURE

Exposure is the amount of light reaching your camera's **sensor** by means of **Aperture**, **Shutter** speed, and **ISO** settings. We will cover sensors later.

Below is the Exposure Pyramid showing how aperture, shutter speed, and ISO make up an exposure.

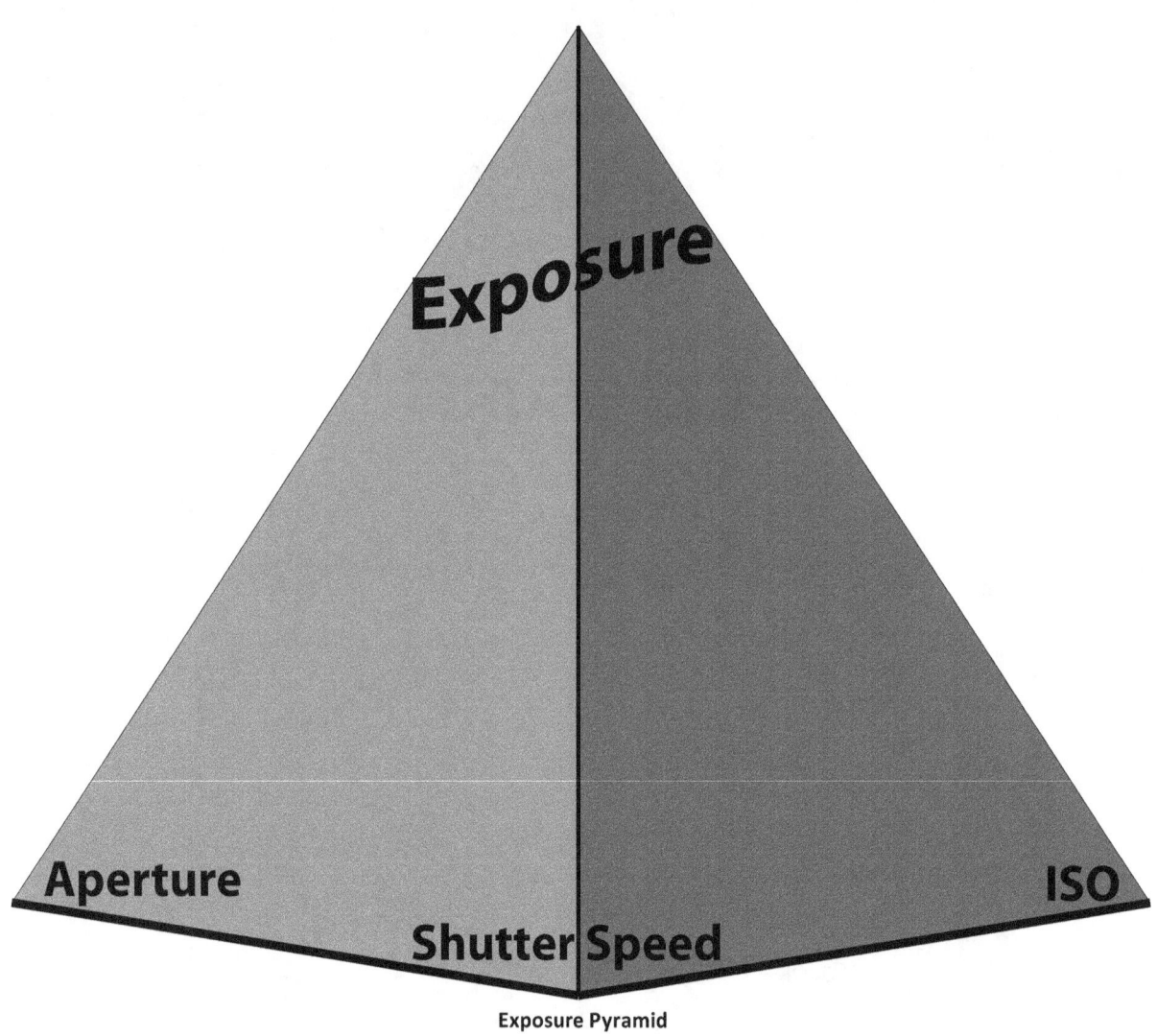

Exposure Pyramid

When the aperture, shutter speed, and ISO settings generate a constant amount of light it is known as **exposure**. The key term here is **constant amount of light**. Aperture and shutter speed is denoted by **exposure value (EV)**. When ISO sensitivity is taken into account the trio is referred to as **Light Value (LV)**. To keep everything simple, light value is encompassed into exposure value. The aperture, shutter speed, and ISO settings can be manipulated in many ways to produce a variety of exposure settings.

If the Aperture is made wider (smaller f number) then the Shutter Speed must be faster to compensate for the wide opening. That is, because the opening of the lens is larger, more light is entering the camera so the shutter quickly opens and closes to reduce the light entering the camera. If a photographer makes the aperture smaller (larger f number) then he must also slow down the shutter speed to maintain consistency. That is, because the opening of the lens is smaller, less light is entering the camera so the shutter stays open longer to obtain more light.

Aperture

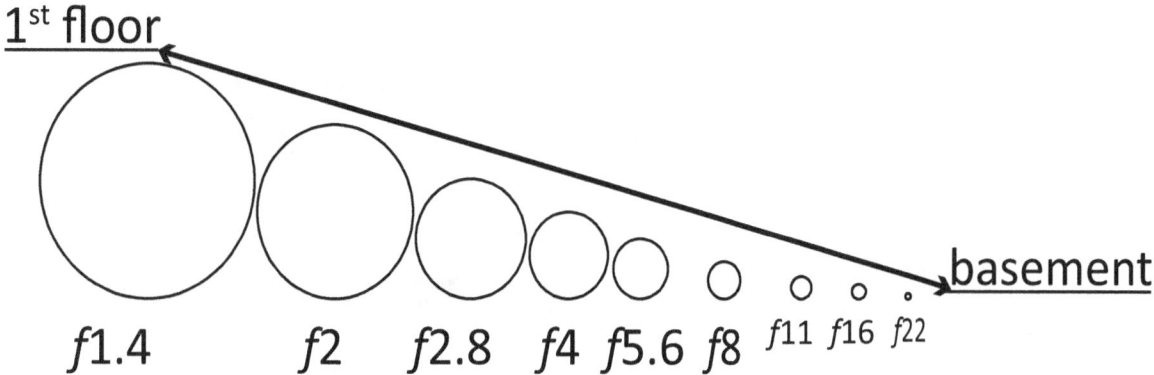

Shutter Speed

Aperture and Shutter Speed

If the ISO is fixed, then for any change in aperture there should be a change in shutter speed to maintain a constant exposure value. Likewise, if the ISO is fixed, then for any change in shutter speed there should be a change in aperture to maintain a constant exposure value. The chart below demonstrates this concept.

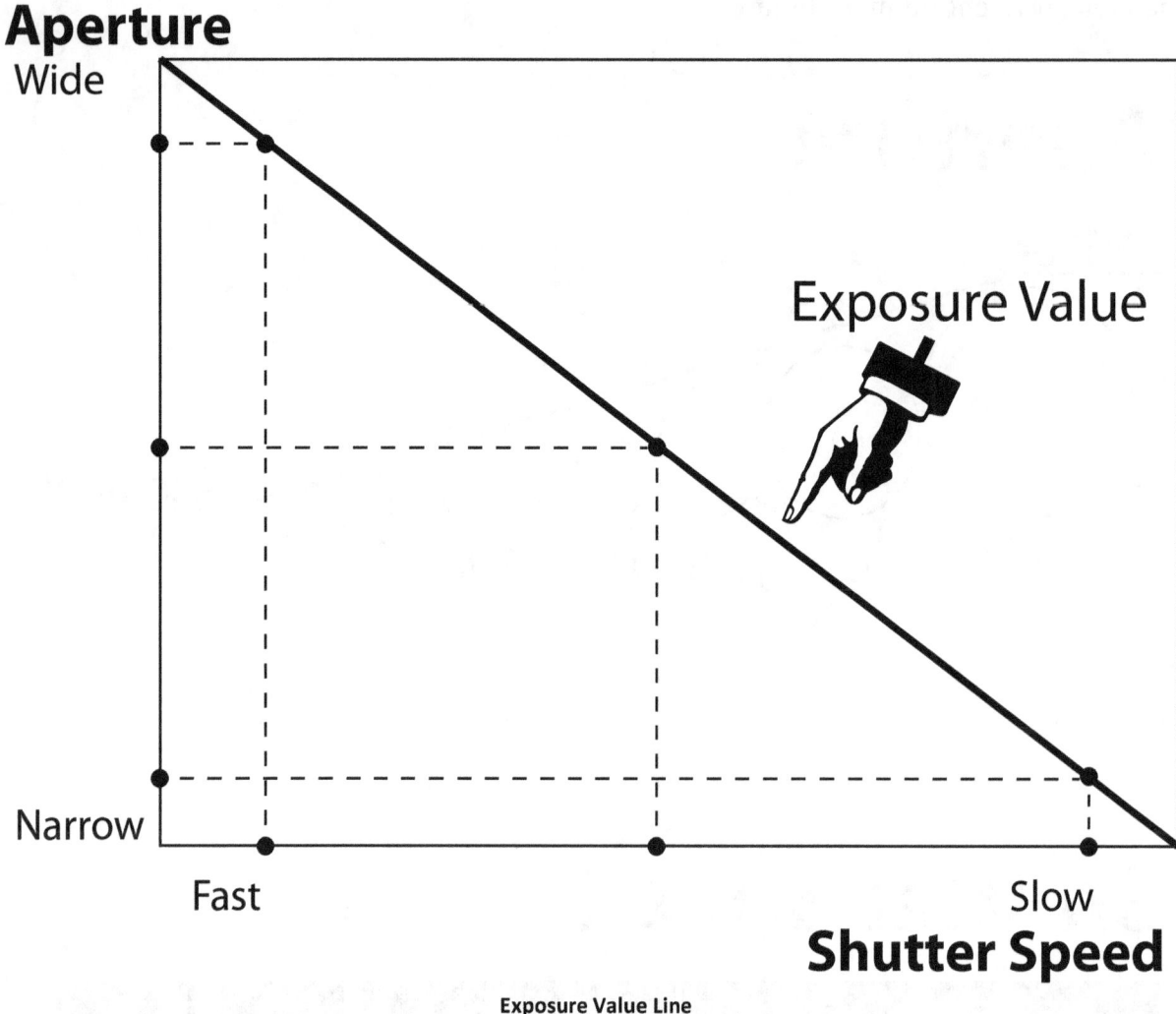

Exposure Value Line

The **exposure value line** extends from the top left corner to the bottom right corner, and the exposure value of any point on this line is constant. The **Aperture** is listed on the **Y axis** and the **Shutter Speed** is listed on the **X axis**. The aperture and shutter speed intersect the exposure value line in three different places on the chart above. The exposure value (**EV**) of all three points is the same, but each point gives a different photograph. That is, if you select the aperture first then adjust the shutter speed you can control **depth of field**. But, if you select the shutter speed first then adjust the aperture you can control **movement**. Before showing an exposure example we will review aperture and shutter speed in terms of **LIGHT**.

Aperture and light:

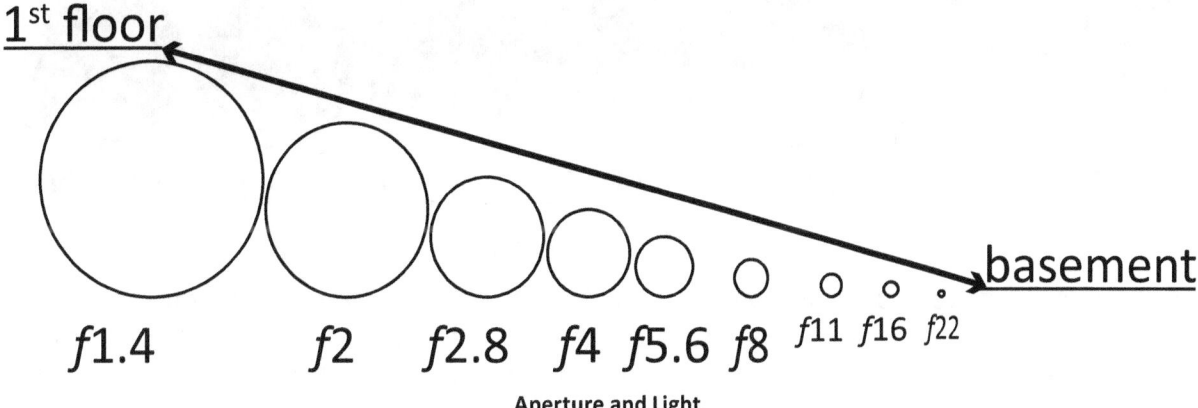

Aperture and Light

The amount of light entering the camera from f2.8 to f4 is cut in half.
The amount of light entering the camera from f4 to f5.6 is cut in half.
The amount of light entering the camera from f5.6 to f8 is cut in half.
The amount of light entering the camera from f8 to f11 is cut in half.

The amount of light entering the camera from f11 to f8 is doubled.
The amount of light entering the camera from f8 to f5.6 is doubled.
The amount of light entering the camera from f5.6 to f4 is doubled.
The amount of light entering the camera from f4 to f2.8 is doubled.

Shutter Speed and light:

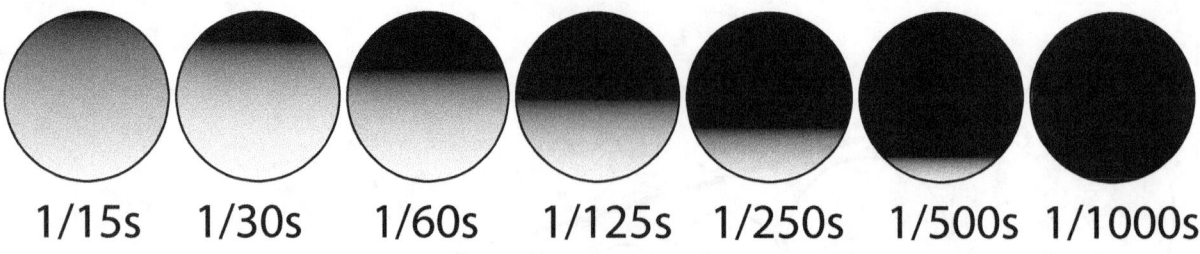
Shutter Speed and light

The longer a shutter speed is opened then the more time light has to enter into the camera. Imagine you have 7 different cameras, each set with a different shutter speed. The camera with the 1/15s shutter is to the far left and the camera with the 1/1000s shutter is to the far right. At 1/15s, the far right shutter is already closed. At 1/1000s, the far left shutter is still opened.

The amount of light entering the camera from 1/15s to 1/30s is cut in half.
The amount of light entering the camera from 1/30s to 1/60s is cut in half.
The amount of light entering the camera from 1/60s to 1/125s is cut in half.
The amount of light entering the camera from 1/125s to 1/250s is cut in half.

The amount of light entering the camera from 1/250s to 1/125s is doubled.
The amount of light entering the camera from 1/125s to 1/60s is doubled.
The amount of light entering the camera from 1/60s to 1/30s is doubled.
The amount of light entering the camera from 1/30s to 1/15s is doubled.

A photographer will measure the correct exposure needed for a scene. After the correct exposure is measured the photographer can use any combination of aperture and shutter speed to obtain the desired amount of light. In layman's terms, if we double the light of one variable then we must take half the light of another variable. Or, if we take half the light of one variable then we must double the other variable. For example, if we double the light for the aperture then we must take half of the current shutter speed light. Likewise, if we double the light of the shutter speed then we must take half the current aperture light, etc.

Suppose you measure an exposure to have an aperture of f8 and a shutter speed of 1/125s. Any of the combinations below will give the correct exposure.

Aperture	f2.8	f4	f5.6	**f8**	f11	f16	f22
Shutter Speed	1/1000s	1/500s	1/250s	**1/125s**	1/60s	1/30s	1/15s

Correct Exposure f8 at 1/125s

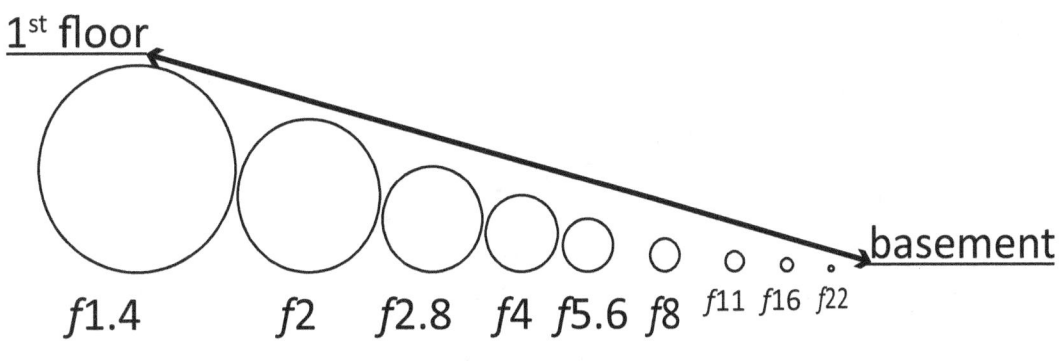

Stairs Diagram for Aperture

If we stop down our aperture from f8 to f11, we use the shutter speed of 1/60s because:
    The amount of light entering the camera from f8 to f11 is cut in half.
    The amount of light entering the camera from 1/125s to 1/60s is doubled.
    We have maintained equality.

If we open up our aperture from f8 to f5.6, we use the shutter speed of 1/250s because:
    The amount of light entering the camera from f8 to f5.6 is doubled.
    The amount of light entering the camera from 1/125s to 1/250s is cut in half.
    We have maintained equality.

If we decrease the shutter speed from 1/125s to 1/60s, we use aperture f11 because:
    The amount of light entering the camera from 1/125s to 1/60s is doubled.
    The amount of light entering the camera from f8 to f11 is cut in half.
    We have maintained equality.

If we increase the shutter speed from 1/125s to 1/250s, we use aperture f5.6 because:
    The amount of light entering the camera from 1/125s to 1/250s is cut in half.
    The amount of light entering the camera from f8 to f5.6 is doubled.
    We have maintained equality.

Exposure in Action

Tools needed:
   none

Suppose you take an exposure measurement and the correct exposure needed is f2.8 at 1/1000s. You decide to shoot your image with an f5.6 instead.

Aperture	**f2.8**	f4	**f5.6**	f8	f11	f16	f22
Shutter Speed	**1/1000s**	1/500s	1/250s	1/125s	1/60s	1/30s	1/15s

Correct Exposure f2.8 at 1/1000s in Action

1. What shutter speed is needed?
2. Why?
3. Use the charts below to help you.

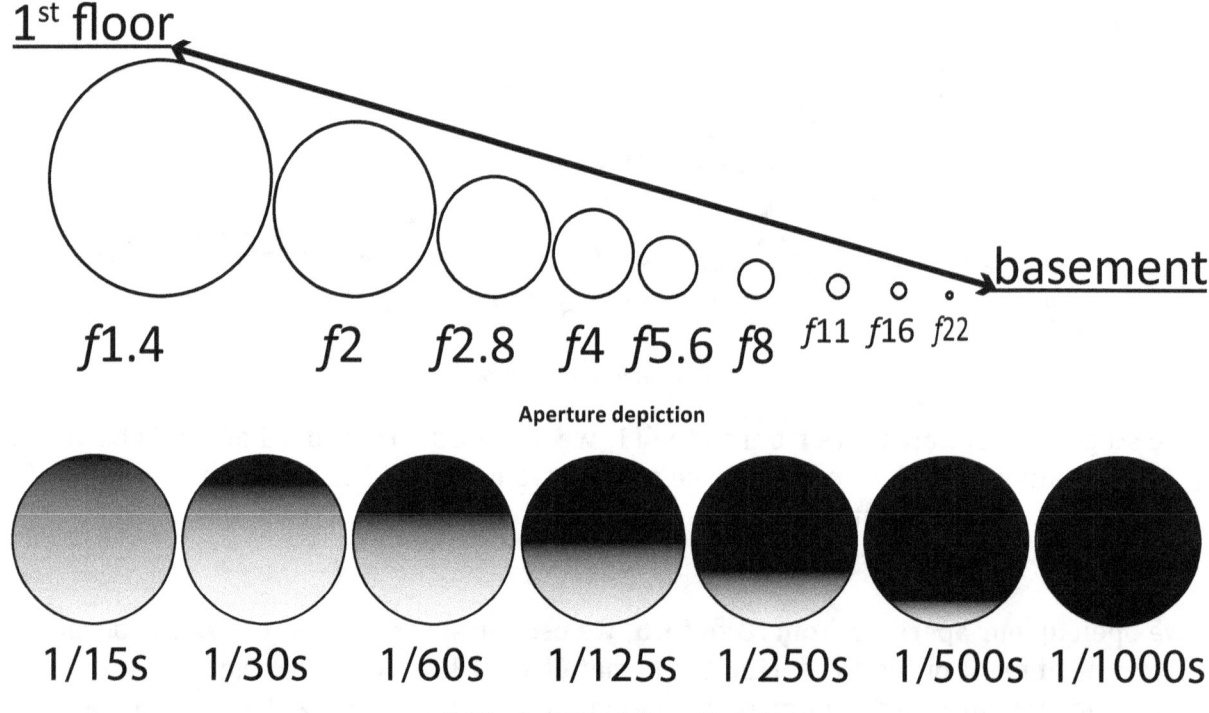

ANSWER BELOW

The shutter speed needed is 1/250s.

This speed is needed because we stopped down the aperture twice losing two full stops of light when going from f2.8 to f5.6. Each stop cuts the light in half. Since we cut the light in half on two occasions we must double the light, twice. If we double the light once we are at 1/500s. When we double the light the second time we have 1/250s. Therefore, f5.6 with shutter speed 1/250s provides the correct exposure. In summary, we stopped down two stops on the aperture so we had to slow the shutter speed down by two stops which kept the shutter opened longer to allow more light to enter the camera.

Exposure Assignment

Tools needed:
   none

Suppose you take an exposure measurement and the correct exposure needed is f5.6 at 1/250s. You decide to shoot your image with shutter speed 1/1000s instead.

Aperture	f2.8	f4	**f5.6**	f8	f11	f16	f22
Shutter Speed	**1/1000s**	1/500s	**1/250s**	1/125s	1/60s	1/30s	1/15s

Correct Exposure f5.6 at 1/250s Assignment

   1. What will be the aperture needed?
   2. Why?
   3. Use the charts below to help you.

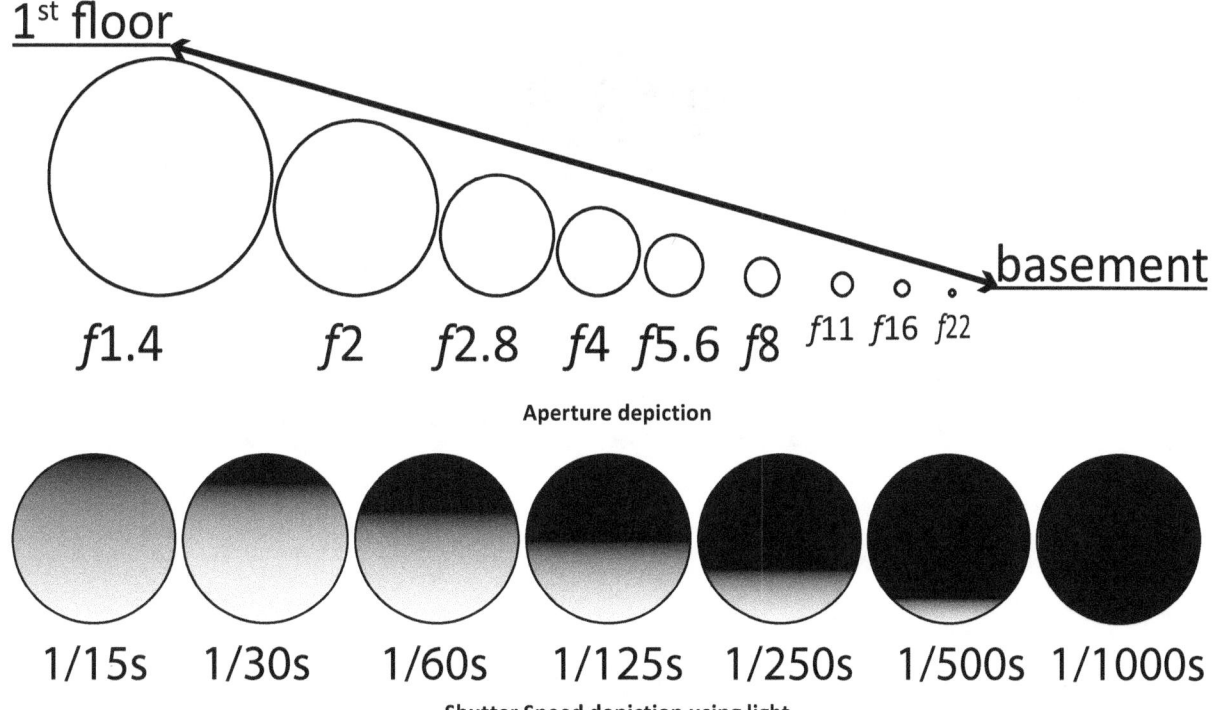

ANSWER BELOW

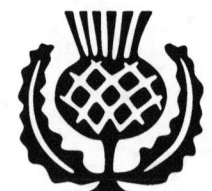

EXPOSURE COMPENSATION

Many cameras have auto-exposure systems which will automatically produce photographs with optimal brightness. Optimal brightness is also known as **optimal exposure**. If a photograph is **too dark** it is **underexposed**. If a photograph is **too bright** it is **overexposed**.

As a photographer you might chose to override the automatic **exposure value** (EV) of your camera so that your images will be overexposed (brighter) or underexposed (darker). That is, **exposure compensation** can be used, for example, to make your shadows lighter or the sky darker.

Exposure Compensation values might range from -5 to 5, in increments of ½ or 1/3rd. In general, negative values make the images darker and positive values make the images lighter. The more negative the number then the more underexposed the image will be. Underexposed means the image is not exposed to enough light. The more positive the number then the more overexposed the image will be. Overexposed means the image is exposed to too much light. When no exposure adjustment is made the EV equals 0 (see image below).

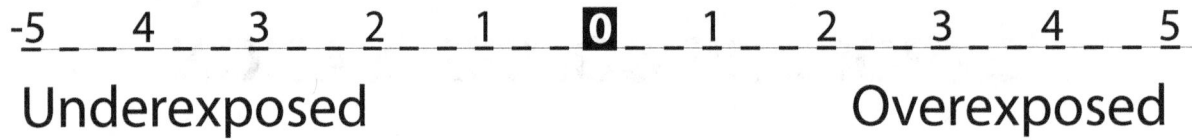

Underexposed and Overexposed line graph

Exposure Compensation is usually stated in terms of **Exposure Value (EV)** units. That is, 1EV unit is one exposure step (stop) which is the doubling and halving of light. From 0 to +3 is three EV units or 3 stops of light. From 0 to -5 is five EV units or 5 stops of light.

With Exposure Compensation, the photographer has the prerogative of underexposing, or overexposing, at only one EV. In other words, a photographer may decide to underexpose at an EV of -5 and make no other exposure adjustments. Likewise, the photographer may decide to underexpose at an EV of -5, and to overexpose at an EV of 2. Thus it is appropriate to say that Exposure Compensation varies the camera's exposure over one, or more, photographs. In the next section you learn about **bracketing** where more than one (a series) exposure adjustments are required. Afterwards we will study the **Histogram** which is a pictorial image on exposure values.

In aperture priority mode, exposure compensation will vary the shutter speed.
In shutter speed priority mode, exposure compensation will vary the aperture.
In program mode, exposure compensation will vary the shutter speed and/or the aperture.
In manual mode, exposure compensation does not apply.

> **Important**: save your images from the exposure compensation assignment in this chapter as the images will also be used for the histogram assignment.

EXPOSURE COMPENSATION IN ACTION

Tools needed:
- Any subject or object
- Yellow highlighter
- Camera
- Tripod
- User guide

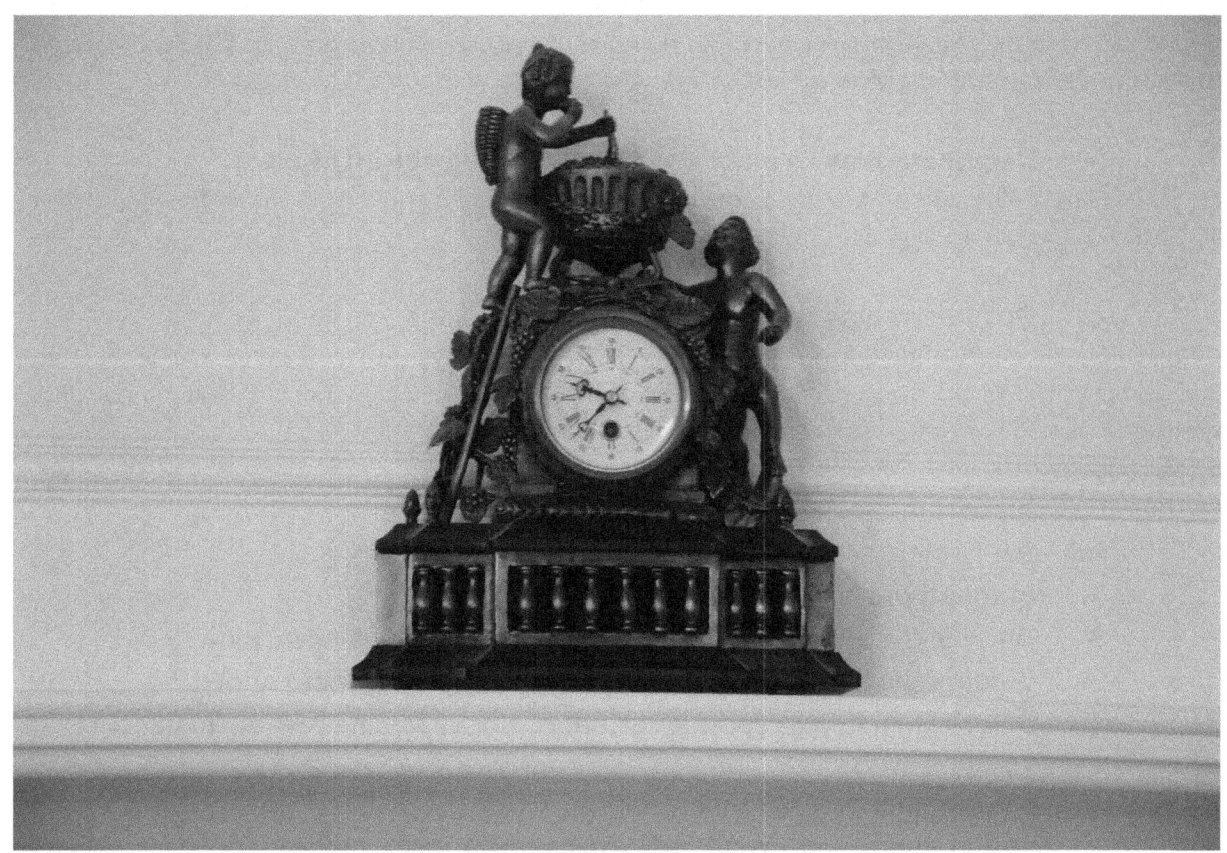

EV 0 (no exposure compensation)

ACCESSING IMAGE INFORMATION

This assignment will require accessing image information. To access the F number, Exposure time, ISO, and Focal Length, do the following:

- **MAC**: right click the file, select *Get Info*, then click the down arrow under *More Info*. You will need your camera's software to see the ISO settings on a MAC.
- **PC**: right click the file, select *Properties*, click the *Details* tab, scroll down to Camera.

Things to Note

For demonstration purposes, 5 exposure adjustments are made. Remember when using exposure compensation, it is optional for a photographer to make more than one exposure adjustment.

STEPS for Exposure Compensation in Action

1. **Document how to access your camera's Exposure Compensation settings:**

On the Nikon D7100: Press the +/- button on the top of the camera. With this button still pressed, rotate the <u>Main Command dial</u> to the right to overexpose (make lighter) and to the left to underexpose (make darker).

2. **Document how to set camera back to normal exposure:**

On the Nikon D7100: power the camera On/Off, press the +/- button on the top of the camera. With this button still pressed, rotate the <u>Main Command dial</u>. If in the negative area then rotate to the right to get to 0. If in the positive area then rotate to the left to get to 0.

3. **Document how to place your camera in Program Mode:**

On the Nikon D7100, press the <u>Mode dial lock release</u> button (top of camera) and rotate the mode dial to P. The P should be aligned to the white dot.

4. **Document how to Manually Focus your Lens:**

On the Nikon D7100: Move the Focus-Mode selector to M. The Focus-Mode selector is on the front of the camera and has the letters AF and M stamped above it. To manually focus the lens, adjust the lens's focusing ring until the image is clear. The focusing ring is behind the zoom area of the lens.

5. Place camera on a **tripod**.
6. Set Camera to **Programmed Mode**.
7. **Manually** focus on a subject/object of your choice.
8. What is the lowest EV (for underexposure) your camera allows? -5
9. What is the highest EV (for overexposure) your camera allows? +5
10. Do not change your focal length nor refocus for the rest of this assignment.
11. Take a photo of your subject/object at EV 0.
12. Take a photo at the following EV; -2, -1, 1, 2.
13. Print, Cut, and Paste the -2 EV in the top box and the +2 EV in the bottom box on the next page.
14. Document your findings, of both images, below that image. Make sure response is in reference to EV 0.
15. Document the **File name**, **EV**, **F number**, **Exposure time**, **ISO**, and **Focal Length**, of each image (from most negative to most positive).
16. **Highlight** the **EV 0** on the Image Information page using a marker.
17. At the bottom of the page, draw an **EV line graph** based on your camera's lowest and highest EV options. [Your graph numbers should match steps 8 & 9]
18. Set the camera back to normal exposure (**EV 0**).
19. **Overview**: Explain in your own words what is happening based on the image information data (and photos).

UNDEREXPOSED AND OVEREXPOSED IMAGES

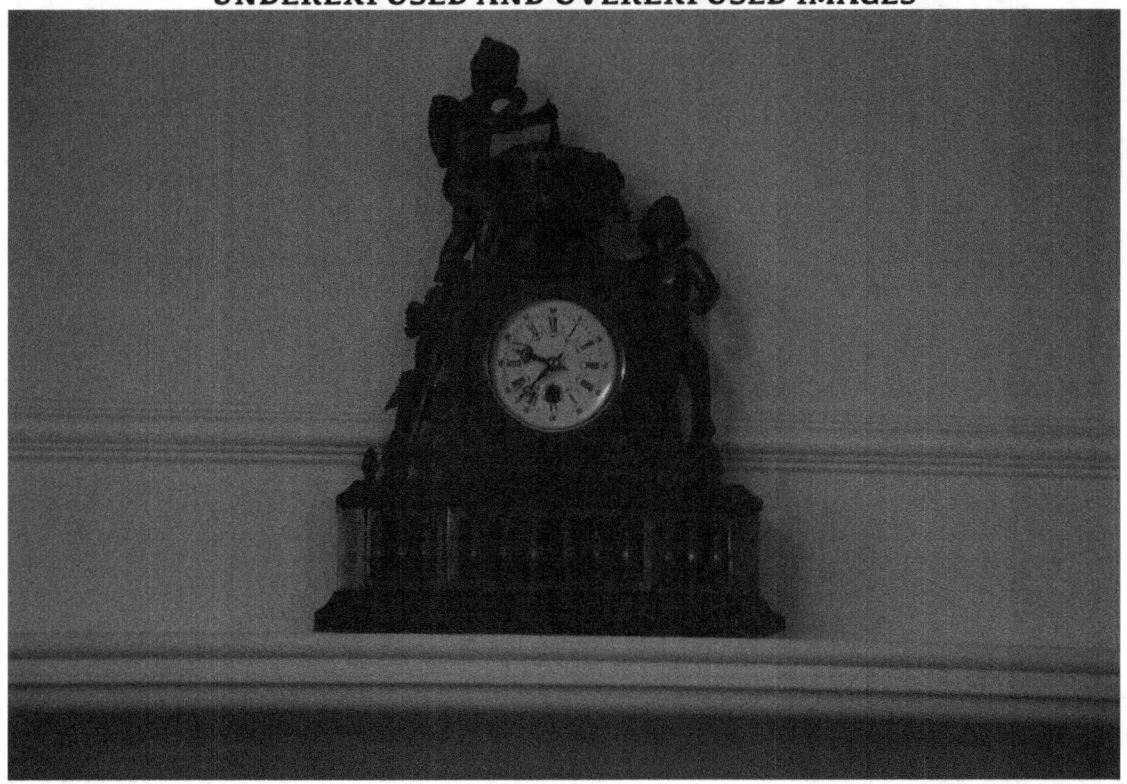

EV -2

At -2EV the light entering the camera decreases (cut in half twice) causing the image to be darker than the image taken at EV0. I can hear the shutter opening and closing quickly.

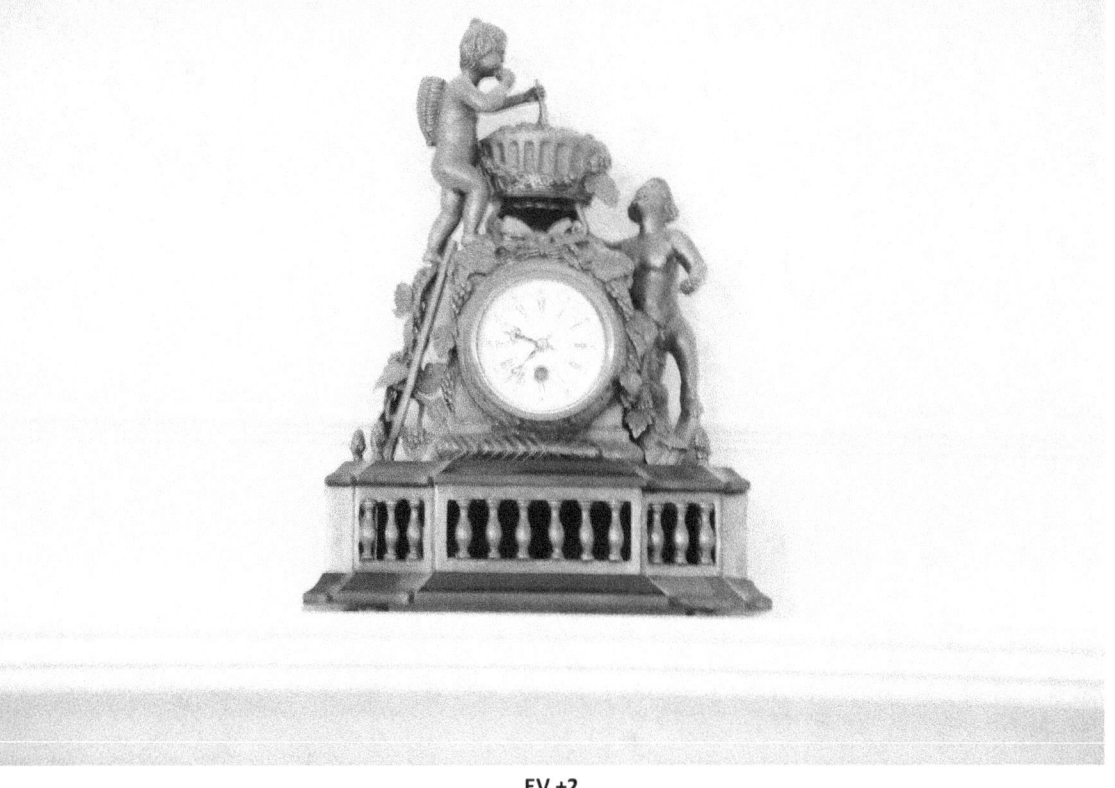

EV +2

At +2EV the light entering the camera increases (doubles twice) causing the image to be lighter than the image taken at EV 0. In order to let in more light the shutter remained opened longer.

IMAGE INFORMATION

File name	EV	F-Number	Exposure Time (Shutter Speed)	ISO	Focal Length
DSC_500.jpg	-2	f5.3	1/3s	100	80mm
DSC_501.jpg	-1	f5.3	1/1.6s	100	80mm
DSC_502.jpg	0	f5.3	1.3s	100	80mm
DSC_503.jpg	+1	f5.3	2.5s	100	80mm
DSC_504.jpg	+2	f5.3	5s	100	80mm

Exposure Compensation Image Information

EV Line Graph

-5 _ _ 4 _ _ 3 _ _ 2 _ _ 1 _ _ **0** _ _ 1 _ _ 2 _ _ 3 _ _ 4 _ _ 5

Underexposed   **Overexposed**

Underexposed and Overexposed line graph

OVERVIEW

In Program Mode the camera decided the optimal exposure (at EV0) was at f5.3 and 1.3 seconds. The ISO, focal length, and aperture remained constant throughout the test.

The more negative the EV then the darker the resulting images; the images were underexposed. The more positive the EV then the lighter the resulting images; the images were overexposed.

The amount of light entering the camera was determined by the speed of the shutter.

At EV -2 the shutter remained open for a short duration of time. Because the shutter was not opened longer a small amount of light entered the camera causing the image to be darker, underexposed.

At EV -1 the shutter opened and closed slightly slower than EV -2 yet still faster than EV 0. Hence the image at EV -1 was darker than EV 0 yet lighter than EV -2.

EV 0 is what the camera considered to be optimal exposure.

At EV +1 the shutter remained open for 1.3 seconds which is a long time in terms of photography. More light had time to enter the camera hence making the photo brighter.

At EV +2 the shutter remained open for 5 seconds. This allowed a lot of light to enter the camera hence overexposing the image.

EXPOSURE COMPENSATION ASSIGNMENT

Tools needed:
    Any subject or object
    Yellow highlighter
    Camera
    Tripod
    User guide

> Optionally print and place your EV 0 here as a 4x6 image.

EV 0

ACCESSING IMAGE INFORMATION
This assignment will require accessing image information. To access the F number, Exposure time, ISO, and Focal Length, do the following:

- **MAC**: right click the file, select *Get Info*, then click the down arrow under *More Info*. You will need your camera's software to see the ISO settings on a MAC.
- **PC**: right click the file, select *Properties*, click the *Details* tab, scroll down to Camera.

Things to Note
For demonstration purposes, 5 exposure adjustments are made. Remember when using exposure compensation, it is optional for a photographer to make more than one exposure adjustment.

Steps for Exposure Compensation Assignment

1. **Document how to access your camera's Exposure Compensation settings:**

2. **Document how to set camera back to normal exposure:**

3. **Document how to place your camera in Program Mode:**

4. **Document how to Manually Focus your Lens:**

5. Place camera on a **tripod**.
6. Set Camera to **Programmed Mode**.
7. **Manually** focus on a subject/object of your choice.
8. What is the lowest EV (for underexposure) your camera allows?_____
9. What is the highest EV (for overexposure) your camera allows? _____
10. Do not change your focal length nor refocus for the rest of this assignment.
11. Take a photo of your subject/object at EV 0.
12. Take a photo at the following EV; -2, -1, 1, 2.
13. Print, Cut, and Paste the -2 EV in the top box and the +2 EV in the bottom box on the next page.
14. Document your findings, of both images, below that image. Make sure response is in reference to EV 0.
15. Document the **File name**, **EV**, **F number**, **Exposure time**, **ISO**, and **Focal Length**, of each image (from most negative to most positive).
16. **Highlight** the **EV 0** on the Image Information page using a marker.
17. At the bottom of the page, draw an **EV line graph** based on your camera's lowest and highest EV options. [Your graph numbers should match steps 8 & 9]
18. Set the camera back to normal exposure (**EV 0**).
19. **Overview**: Explain in your own words what is happening based on the image information data (and photos).

UNDEREXPOSED AND OVEREXPOSED IMAGES

IMAGE INFORMATION

File name	EV	F-Number	Exposure Time (Shutter Speed)	ISO	Focal Length

EV Line Graph

OVERVIEW

BRACKETING

Bracketing automatically varies the camera's exposure over a **series** of photographs.

In the last section we used Exposure Compensation to vary the exposure. That is, we took a photo, adjusted the exposure, took another photo, adjusted the exposure, then took another photo, and so on in this manner. With bracketing, we tell the camera up front what we desire to do, then snap the image the required amount of times without readjusting between shots.

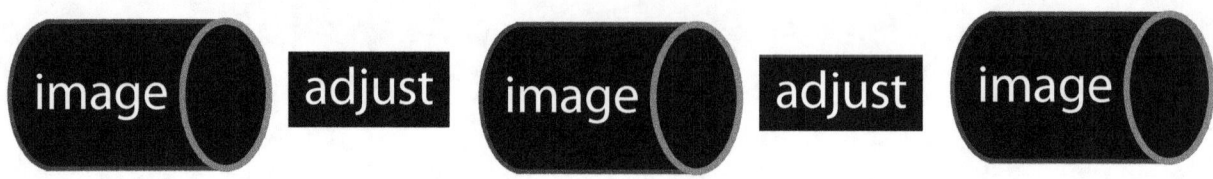

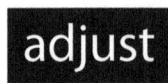 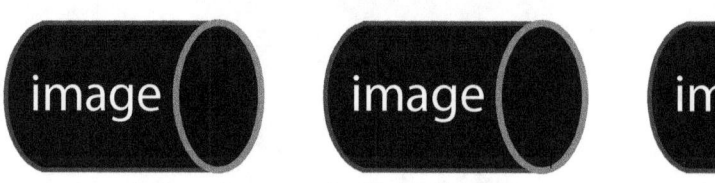

Exposure Compensation vs. Bracketing

The diagram above shows the concept between Exposure Compensation and Bracketing. If a camera offers bracketing it may be in increments of 1/3 EV, ½ EV, or 1 EV.

In decimal format, 1/3 equals .33333 where the 3 is repeating. And, 2/3 equals .666667 rounded up to point 7. Therefore, if you see a 1/3 EV with a point 7 option then you know it is two divided by three rounded up.

Increment of 1/3 EV

-2   -1.7   -1.3   **-1**   -.7   -.3   **0**   .3   .7   **1**   1.3   1.7   **2**

Bracketing 1/3rd increments

Here is a scenario of how 1/3 EV increments might work. A +5F, for example, set to 1/3 EV, means **five images** will be taken (because of the number 5), and the images will go in a positive direction (because of the +). The first image is 0. The second image moves in the positive direction by 1/3 EV which is +.3, and the next image moves in a positive direction by 1/3 EV which is +.7, and so on, until we reach our final image at +1.3. Below are some examples of what you might see.

+5F set to 1/3 EV yields the following images taken at:
0   +.3   +.7   +1   +1.3
Since there is a positive in front of five we move toward the positive end.

5 set to 1/3 EV yields:
0   -.3   +.3   -.7   +.7
Since there is no sign in front of 5 we move on both ends.

-3 set to 1/3 EV yields:
0   -.3   -.7
Since there is a negative in front of three we move toward the negative end.

Here is a scenario of how 1/2 EV increments might work. Every camera is different so check your camera's documentation to determine how to use increments on your camera.

Increment of 1/2 EV

-2   -1.5   **-1**   -.5   **0**   +.5   **1**   +1.5   **2**

Bracketing 1/2 increments

The 1/2 EV increment in decimal format is .5.

3 set to ½ EV yields:
0   +.5   -.5
Since there is no sign in front of 3 we move on both ends.

+3 set to ½ EV yields:
0   +.5   1
Since there is a positive in front of three we move toward the positive end.

-3 set to ½ EV yields:
0   -.5   -1
Since there is a negative in front of three we move toward the negative end.

Please note that every camera is different so check your camera's documentation to determine how to use increments on your camera. If the camera is set for continuous burst shooting the images will be captured quickly which is great for rapidly changing subjects. Bracketing is often used in High Dynamic Range (HDR) imaging. HDR is beyond the scope of this book.

BRACKETING IN ACTION

Tools needed:
- Any subject or object
- Yellow highlighter
- Camera
- Tripod
- User guide

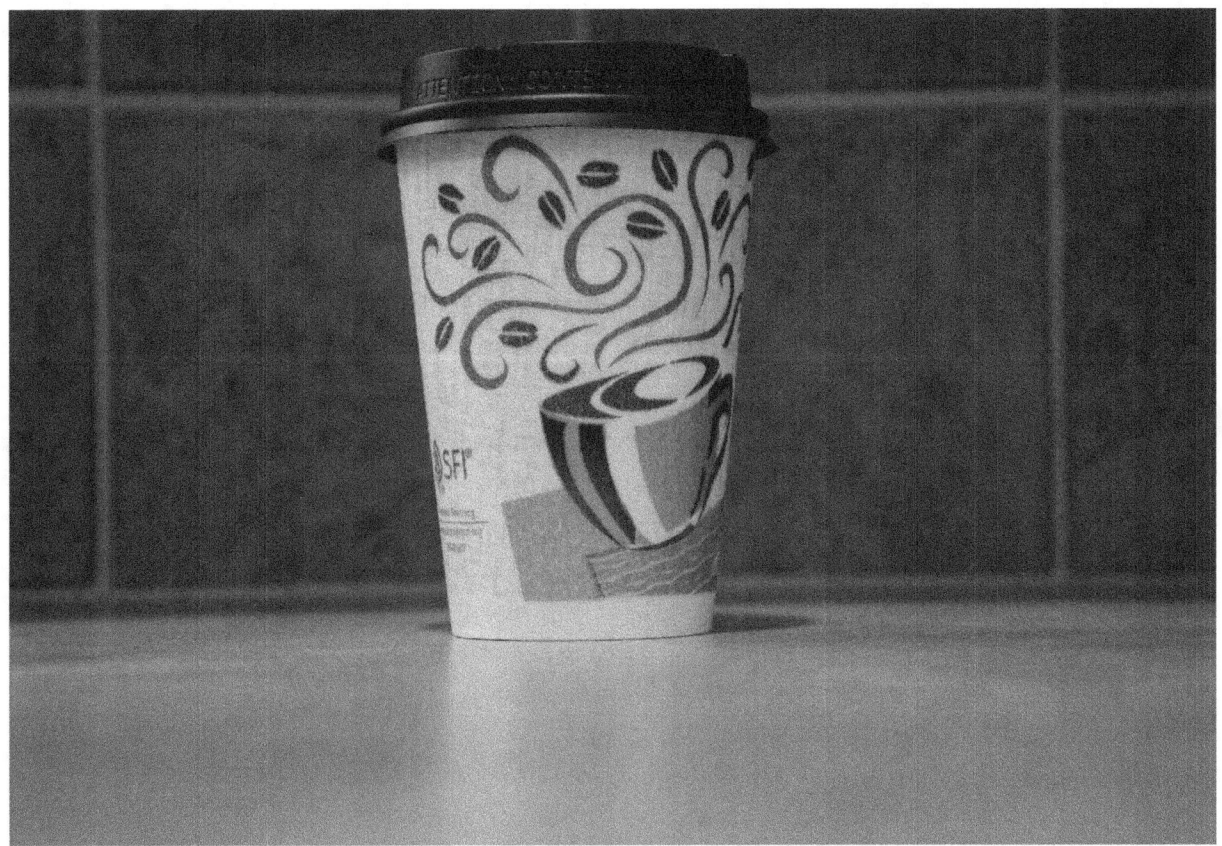

Bracketing Photo taken at EV 0

ACCESSING IMAGE INFORMATION
This assignment will require accessing image information. To access the F number, Exposure time, ISO, and Focal Length, do the following:

- **MAC**: right click the file, select *Get Info*, then click the down arrow under *More Info*. You will need your camera's software to see the ISO settings on a MAC.
- **PC**: right click the file, select *Properties*, click the *Details* tab, scroll down to Camera.

Things to Note
N/A

STEPS for Bracketing in Action

1. **Document how to access your camera's Bracketing Mode settings:**

    On the Nikon D7100:
    a) *Camera setup: Turn on the camera, Press the Menu button on the back of the camera. Scroll to the Pencil tool, select e Bracketing/flash, Select e6 Auto bracketing set, Select AE AE only, press OK.*
    b) *Choose number of shots: Press the BKT button on the front left of the camera. Rotate the main command dial on the back of the camera to chose the number of shots in the bracketing sequence. (Listed as #F, where # is a number).*
    c) *Select bracketing increment: Press the BKT button on the front left of the camera. Rotate the sub command dial on the front of the camera to chose the bracketing increment. The increments display in the control panel at the top of the camera. A +3F means 3 shots from zero toward the positive end. A -3F means 3 shots from zero toward the negative end.*

2. **Document how to cancel Bracketing:**

    On the Nikon D7100, turn on the camera, press the BKT button, rotate the Main Command dial, on the back of the camera, until the BKT icon and the bracketing progress indicator is no longer displayed.

3. **Document how to place your camera in Program Mode:**

    On the Nikon D7100, press the Mode dial lock release button (top of camera) and rotate the mode dial to P. The P should be aligned to the white dot.

4. **Document how to Manually Focus your Lens:**

    On the Nikon D7100: Move the Focus-Mode selector to M. The Focus-Mode selector is on the front of the camera and has the letters AF and M stamped above it. To manually focus the lens, adjust the lens's focusing ring until the image is clear. The focusing ring is behind the zoom area of the lens.

5. Bracket your camera to take **three shots** at a **1 EV increment** (-1, 0, +1).
6. Place camera on a **tripod**.
7. Set Camera to **Programmed Mode**.
8. **Manually** focus on a subject/object of your choice.
9. Do not change your focal length nor refocus for the rest of this assignment.
10. Take three snapshots.
11. Print, Cut, and Paste the -1 EV in the top box and the +1 EV in the bottom box on the next page.
12. Document your findings, of both images, below that image. Make sure response is in reference to EV 0.
13. Document the **File name**, **EV**, **F number**, **Exposure time**, **ISO**, and **Focal Length**, of each image (from most negative to most positive).
14. **Highlight** the **EV 0** on the Image Information page using a marker.
15. **Cancel bracketing**.
16. **Synopsis**: Beneath the image information table, give a short synopsis of what is happening based on the image information data (and photos). This should be brief.

UNDEREXPOSED AND OVEREXPOSED IMAGES

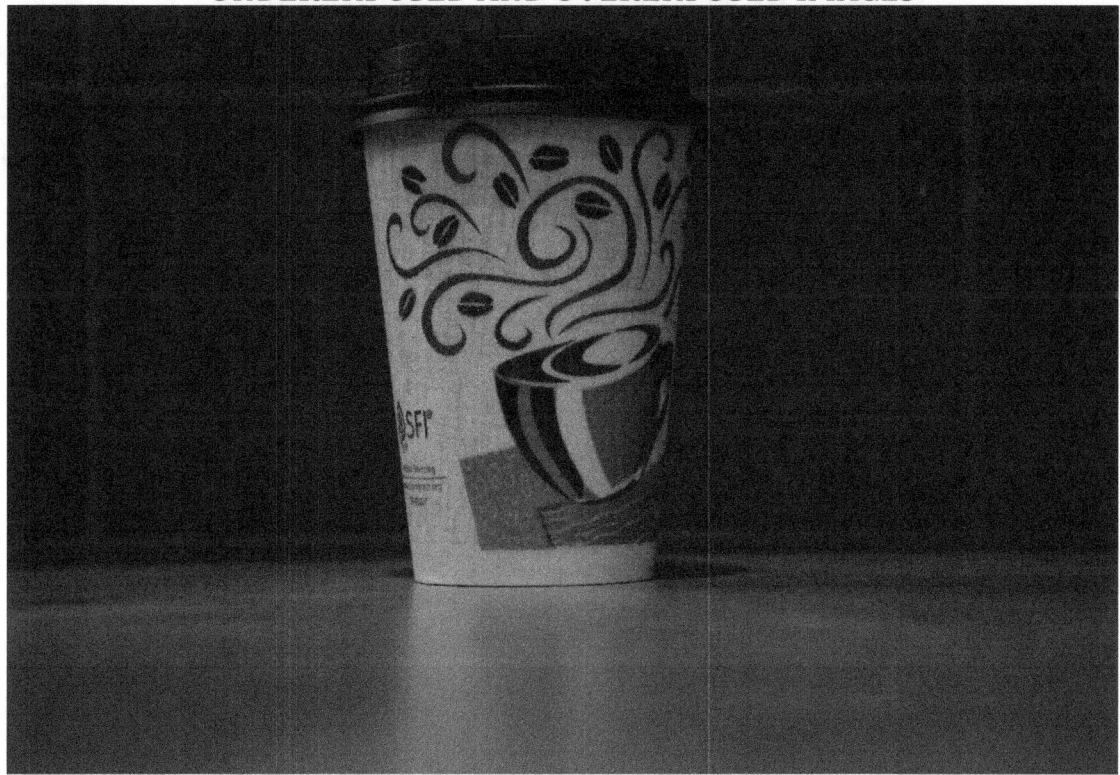

Bracketing EV -1

At -1EV light entering the camera decreases (cut in half) causing the image to be darker than the image taken at EV0.

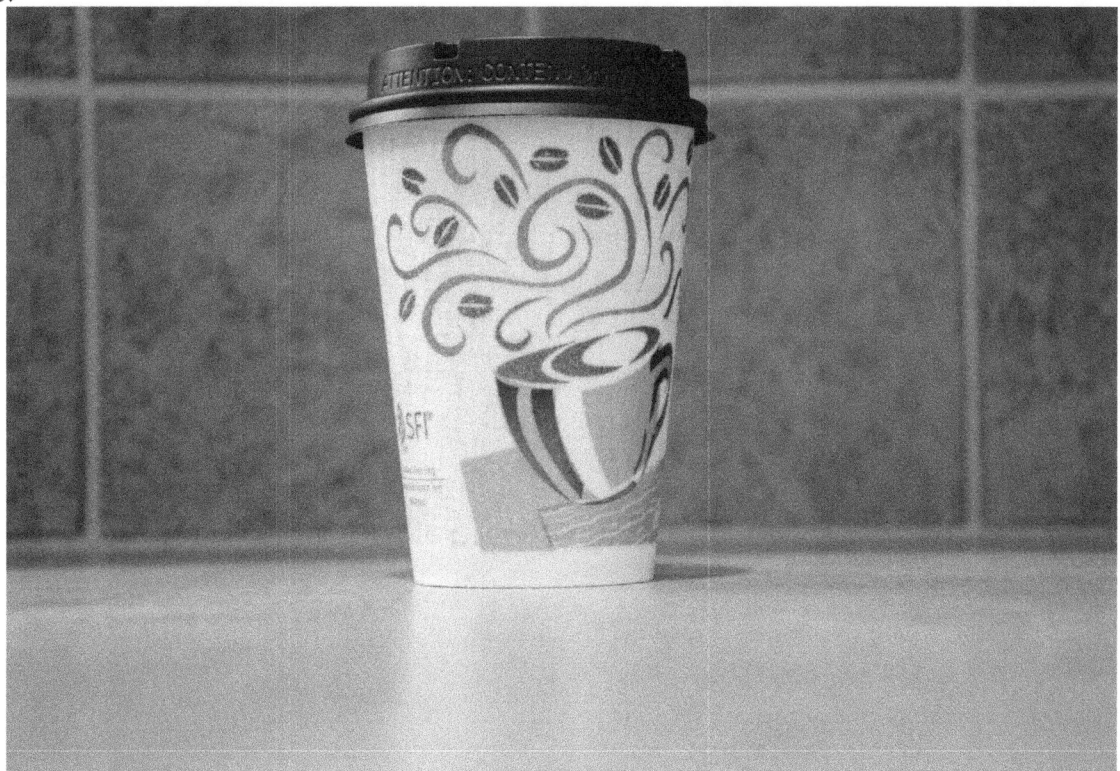

Bracketing EV +1

At +1EV the light entering the camera increases (doubles) causing the image to be lighter than the image taken at EV 0.

IMAGE INFORMATION

File name	EV	F-Number	Exposure Time (Shutter Speed)	ISO	Focal Length
DSC_520.jpg	-1	f4.8	1/4s	100	56mm
DSC_520.jpg	0	f4.8	1/2s	100	56mm
DSC_521.jpg	+1	f4.8	1s	100	56mm

SYNOPSIS

The outcome of what is happening with bracketing is similar to exposure compensation. The main difference is that bracketing will create a series of shots (more than one image) where as exposure compensation will create one image with the option of compensating for more images.

BRACKETING ASSIGNMENT

Tools needed:
- Any subject or object
- Yellow highlighter
- Camera
- Tripod
- User guide

> Optionally print and place your EV 0 here as a 4x6 image.

EV 0

ACCESSING IMAGE INFORMATION

This assignment will require accessing image information. To access the F number, Exposure time, ISO, and Focal Length, do the following:

- **MAC**: right click the file, select *Get Info*, then click the down arrow under *More Info*. You will need your camera's software to see the ISO settings on a MAC.
- **PC**: right click the file, select *Properties*, click the *Details* tab, scroll down to Camera.

Things to Note
N/A

STEPS for Bracketing in Action

1. **Document how to access your camera's Bracketing Mode settings:**

2. **Document how to cancel Bracketing:**

3. **Document how to place your camera in Program Mode:**

4. **Document how to Manually Focus your Lens:**

5. Bracket your camera to take **three shots** at a **1 EV increment** (-1, 0, +1).
6. Place camera on a **tripod**.
7. Set Camera to **Programmed Mode**.
8. **Manually** focus on a subject/object of your choice.
9. Do not change your focal length nor refocus for the rest of this assignment.
10. Take three snapshots.
11. Print, Cut, and Paste the -1 EV in the top box and the +1 EV in the bottom box on the next page.
12. Document your findings, of both images, below that image. Make sure response is in reference to EV 0.
13. Document the **File name**, **EV**, **F number**, **Exposure time**, **ISO**, and **Focal Length**, of each image (from most negative to most positive).
14. **Highlight** the **EV 0** on the Image Information page using a marker.
15. **Cancel bracketing**.
16. **Synopsis**: Beneath the image information table, give a short synopsis of what is happening based on the image information data (and photos). This should be brief.

UNDEREXPOSED AND OVEREXPOSED IMAGES

IMAGE INFORMATION

File name	EV	F-Number	Exposure Time (Shutter Speed)	ISO	Focal Length

SYNOPSIS

HISTOGRAM

A **histogram** shows the distribution of tones in a image. The histogram is only a guide hence the histogram on your camera may slightly differ from the histogram in your computer's imaging software.

It is a good idea to always check your histogram after taking a photo. The histogram may be more important than the actual image if shooting in jpeg as the histogram will show you whether an image is underexposed or overexposed.

If your image is neither too dark nor too light then the histogram tonal range will have a large even distribution.

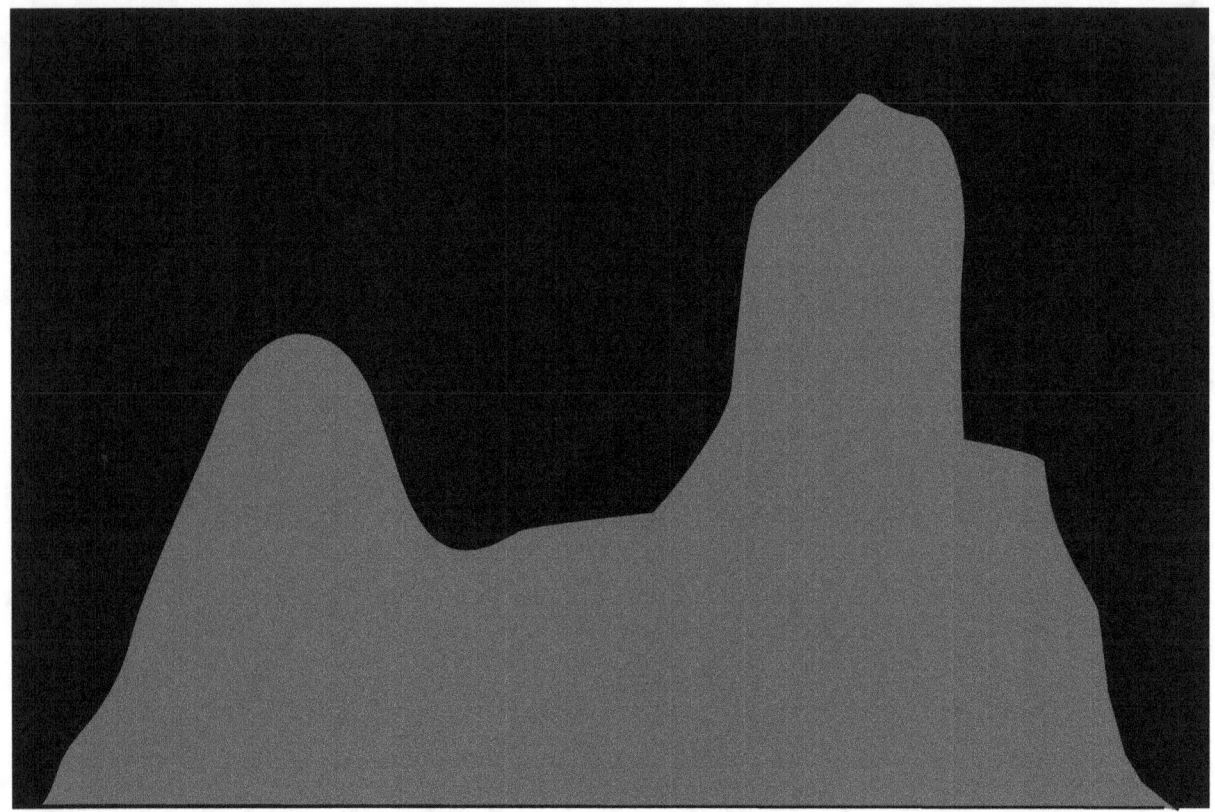

Histogram with Even Tonal Distribution

The Histogram above has no exposure issues.

There are also some RGB histograms. This chapter deals with exposure histograms.

If your histogram shows your image is under or over exposed, then exposure compensation is needed to fix the problem.

-5 _ _ _ 4 _ _ _ 3 _ _ _ 2 _ _ _ 1 _ _ _ **0** _ _ _ 1 _ _ _ 2 _ _ _ 3 _ _ _ 4 _ _ _ 5

Underexposed   Overexposed

Exposure Compensation graph

If your image is too dark (underexposed) then the distribution of tones is shifted to the left as seen on the histogram below. Increasing exposure compensation will shift the tones to the right.

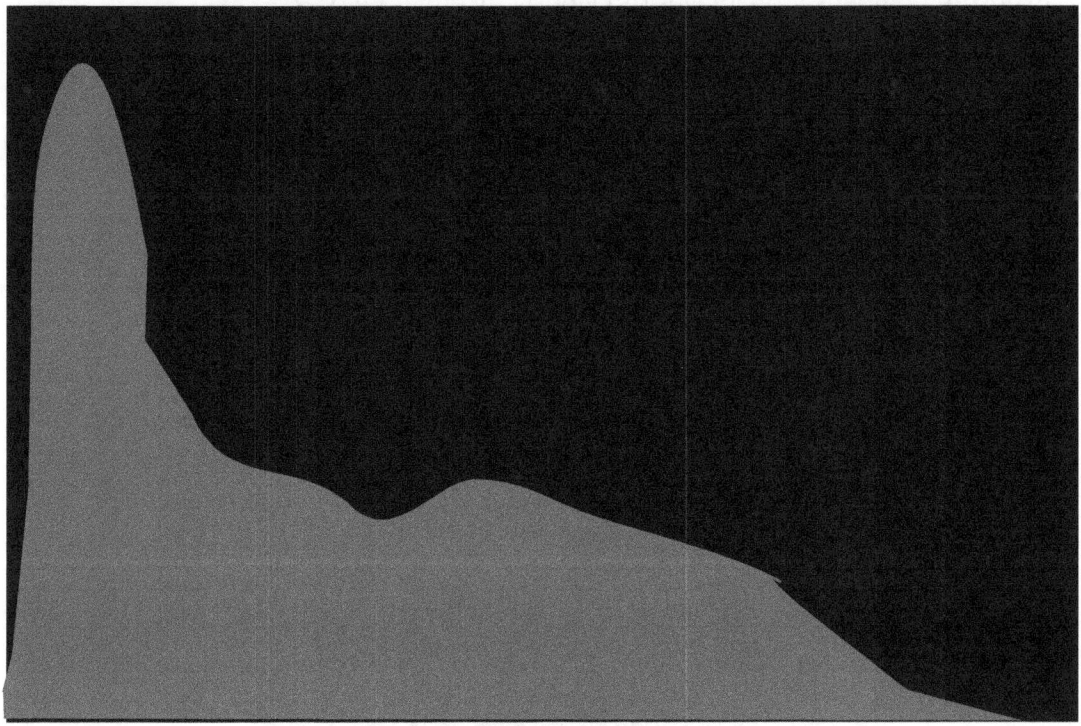

Histogram Underexposed

If your image is too light (overexposed) then the distribution of tones is shifted to the right as seen on the histogram below. Decreasing exposure compensation will shift the tones to the left.

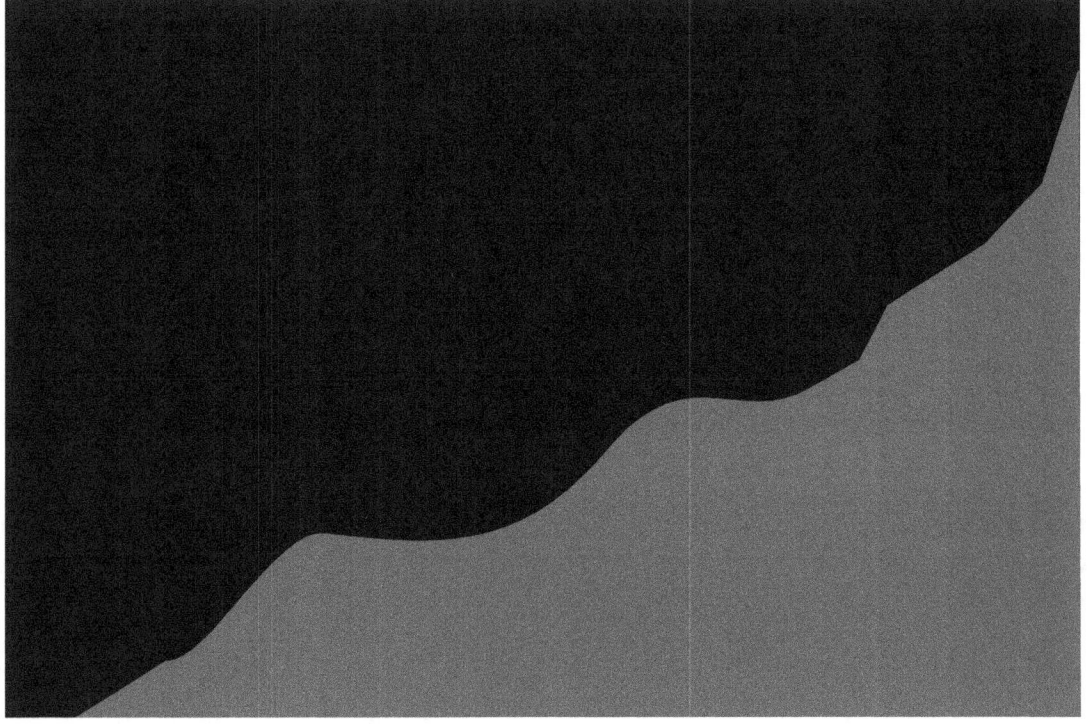

Histogram Overexposed

HISTOGRAM IN ACTION

Tools needed:
Exposure Compensation images (previously taken) at EV 0, -2, +2.

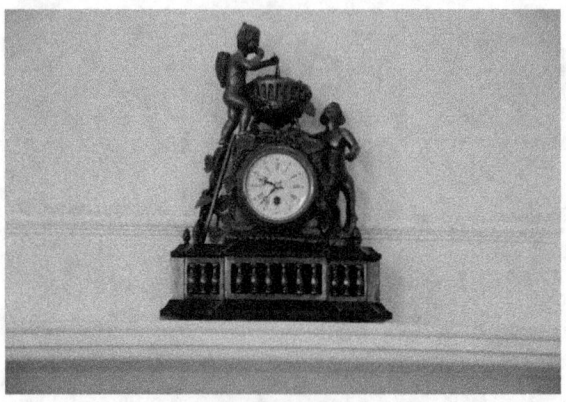
EV 0 image

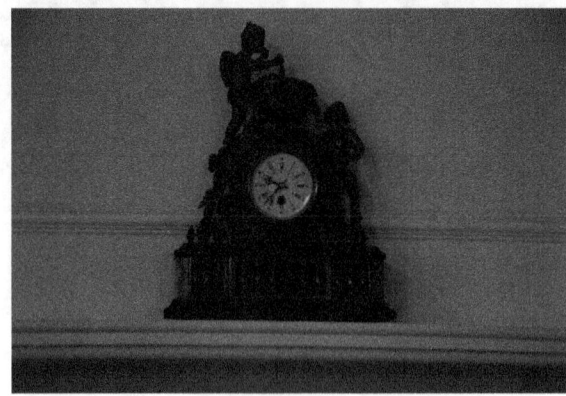
EV -2 image

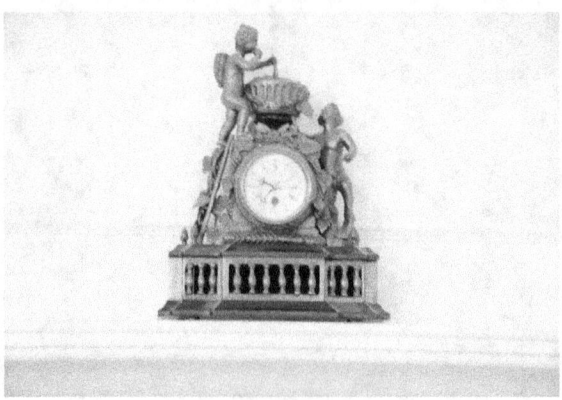
EV +2 image

Things to Note
Histogram information can be viewed on your camera or by using photography software.

114

STEPS for Histogram in Action

1. **Document how to access the histogram view of your image:**

On the computer: Using the ViewNX 2 software by Nikon, find the desired image, make sure the histogram icon is selected in the workspace area.

On the camera: Press the <u>playback button</u> icon (to the direct left of the trash icon). Press the up arrow on the <u>multi selector wheel</u>.

2. Review your exposure compensation images taken at EV 0, EV -2, and EV +2.
3. Hand draw what the histogram looks like at EV 0.
4. Hand draw what the histogram looks like at EV -2.
5. Hand draw what the histogram looks like at EV +2.
6. **Overview**: explain what is happening with the histogram drawings and base a conclusion of what you should do when taking photographs.

HISTOGRAM DRAWINGS

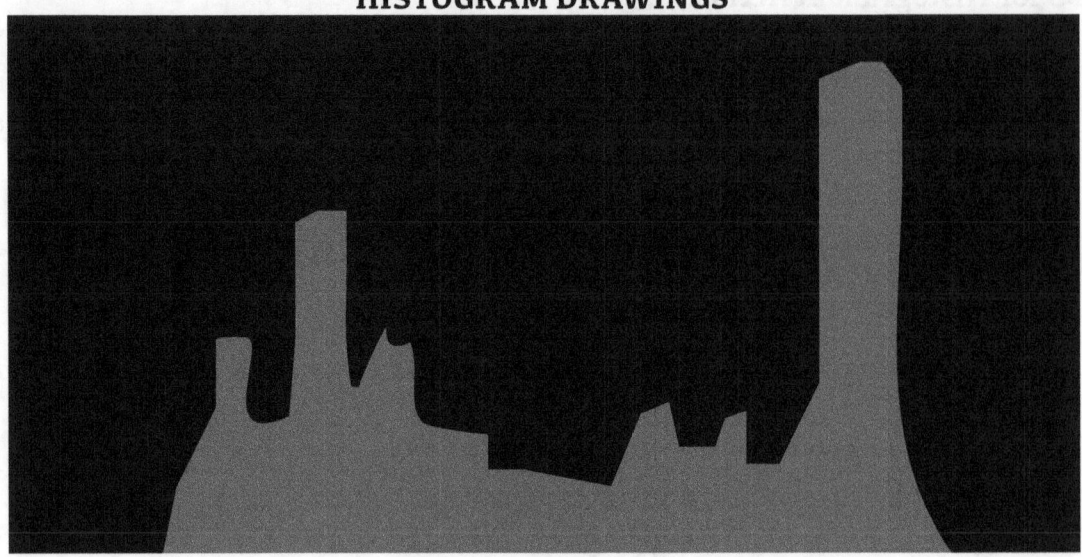

Histogram Drawing at EV 0

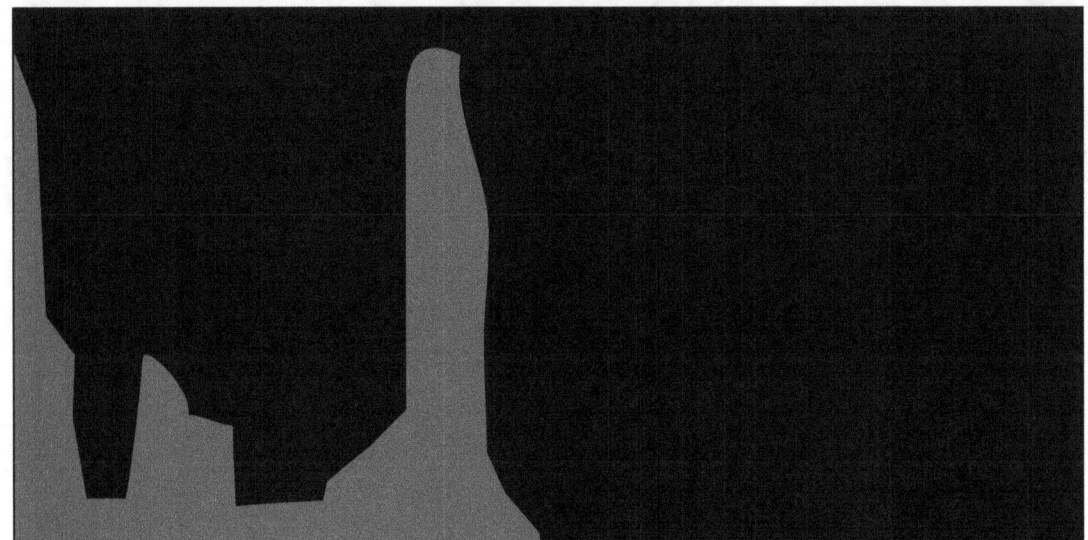

Histogram Drawing at EV -2

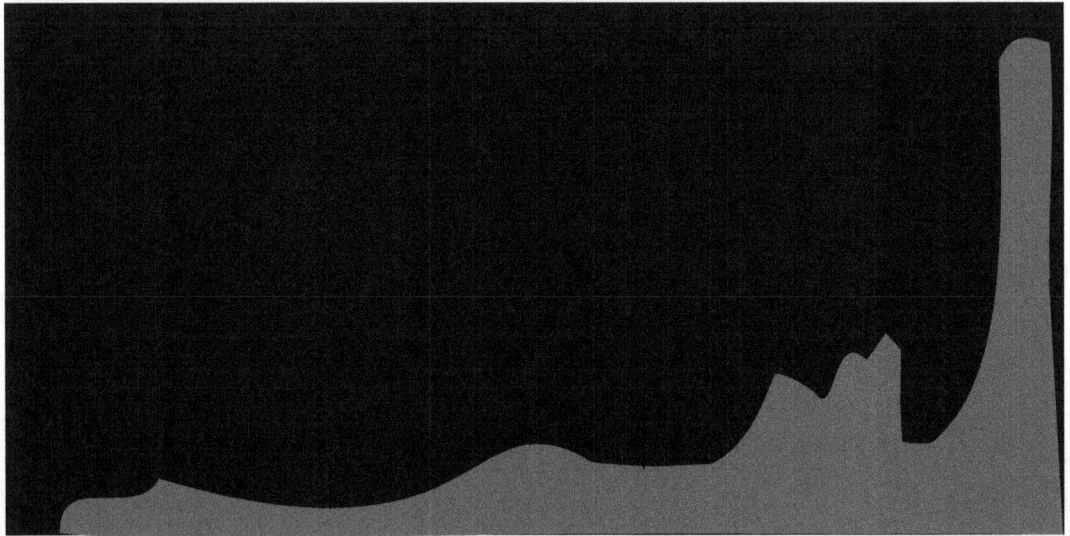

Histogram Drawing EV +2

OVERVIEW

At EV 0 the image is neither underexposed nor overexposed.

At EV -2 the image is underexposed causing the histogram to shift to the left. An underexposed image will be darker than a correctly exposed image.

At EV +2 the image is over exposed causing the histogram to shift to the right. An overexposed image will be lighter than a correctly exposed image.

In conclusion, I recommend taking some test shots with the available light. After each shot one should look at the histogram. If the histogram shows the image is underexposed (too dark) then the exposure compensation should be increased to shift the tones to the right. If the histogram shows the image is overexposed (too light) then the exposure compensation should be decreased to shift the tones to the left. If the histogram shows the image is neither underexposed nor overexposed then no action is required.

HISTOGRAM ASSIGNMENT

Tools needed:
    Exposure Compensation images (previously taken) at EV 0, -2, +2.

Things to Note
Histogram information can be viewed on your camera or by using photography software.

STEPS for Histogram in Action

1. **Document how to access the histogram view of your image:**

2. Review your exposure compensation images taken at EV 0, EV -2, and EV +2.
3. Hand draw what the histogram looks like at EV 0.
4. Hand draw what the histogram looks like at EV -2.
5. Hand draw what the histogram looks like at EV +2.
6. **Overview**: explain what is happening with the histogram drawings and base a conclusion of what you should do when taking photographs.

HISTOGRAM DRAWINGS

Drawing of **EV 0 histogram** below

Drawing of **EV -2 histogram** below

Drawing of **EV +2 histogram** below

OVERVIEW

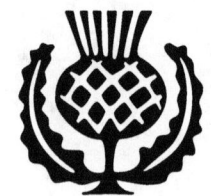

WHITE BALANCE

Different types of light sources put out different hues of light. A white fluorescent light will look differently than a high temperature mercury-vapor light. Likewise, incandescent light looks differently than direct sunlight.

Light color is measured on a temperature scale known as **Kelvin** (K). Lower Kelvin numbers mean the light has a yellower or redder hue and is considered warmer colors. Higher Kelvin numbers mean the light has a whiter or bluer hue and is considered cooler colors.

Images taken in sunlight appear closest to true colors. Images taken under tungsten light appear orange, and images under fluorescent light appear bluish. The latter two instances are examples of why white balance is necessary.

White balance is designed to make the colors in your image accurate. With white balance, you tell the camera what the color white is. This is done by holding up a piece of white paper to your camera.

Without white balance your images might be affected by the color of the light source, and, you may end up with an orange, yellow, or blue tint on your photographs.

Generally you set your camera's white balance to the light source you are using. If you are indoors and the light source is an incandescent light then you set your camera's white balance to incandescent/indoors. If you are outside in direct sunlight then you set your camera's white balance to direct sunlight.

Most digital cameras do an excellent job with automatically adjusting white balance.

WHITE BALANCE IN ACTION

Tools needed:
    Any subject or object
    Yellow highlighter
    Camera
    Tripod
    User guide

Things to Note
White Balance is set based on the source of the light you are photographing your subject in. That is, if you are in daylight and in the shade then you use the shade option or an equivalent based on your camera's user guide.

The next assignment will be done in one of the following lighting conditions: incandescent, fluorescent, direct sunlight, flash, cloudy, or shade. If your camera offers a light source not listed above and you have that light source available then feel free to use it.

STEPS for White Balance in Action

1. **Document how to place your camera in Program Mode:**

On the Nikon D7100, press the <u>Mode dial lock release</u> button (top of camera) and rotate the mode dial to P. The P should be aligned to the white dot.

2. **Document how to access your White Balance settings:**

White balance with the Nikon d7100..
- Place camera in Programmed mode (or any mode other than automatic).
- Press <u>?/key WB</u> button.
- Rotate <u>Main Command dial</u> until the desired white balance option is displayed in the control panel.
- The White Balance options will cycle through the following:
    - AUTO
    - Incandescent
    - Fluorescent
    - Direct sunlight
    - Flash
    - Cloudy
    - Shade
    - Chose color temp.
    - PRE – Preset manual

3. **Document how to Manually Focus your Lens:**

On the Nikon D7100: Move the Focus-Mode selector to M. The Focus-Mode selector is on the front of the camera and has the letters AF and M stamped above it. To manually focus the lens, adjust the lens's focusing ring until the image is clear. The focusing ring is behind the zoom area of the lens.

4. Place camera on a **tripod** pointed toward desired subject/object.
5. Set Camera to **Programmed Mode**.
6. The lighting for your subject should be either incandescent, fluorescent, direct sunlight, flash, cloudy, or shade.
7. What lighting condition are you using? *Direct sunlight*
8. Do not change the lighting conditions for the rest of this assignment.
9. **Manually** focus on a subject/object of your choice.
10. Snap a photo of your subject using **AUTO white balance**.
11. Snap a photo using the White Balance light setting you are using in **question 7**.
12. Snap a photo of the remaining white balance choices in step **#6**.
13. Return the white balance to **AUTO**.
14. Print, Cut, and Paste the **AUTO** white balanced image in the top box and the white balance image from **question 7** in the bottom box on the next page. Document the name of the white balance light source used for the bottom image.
15. **Overview**: Document your findings for step #12.

AUTO WHITE BALANCE AND OTHER

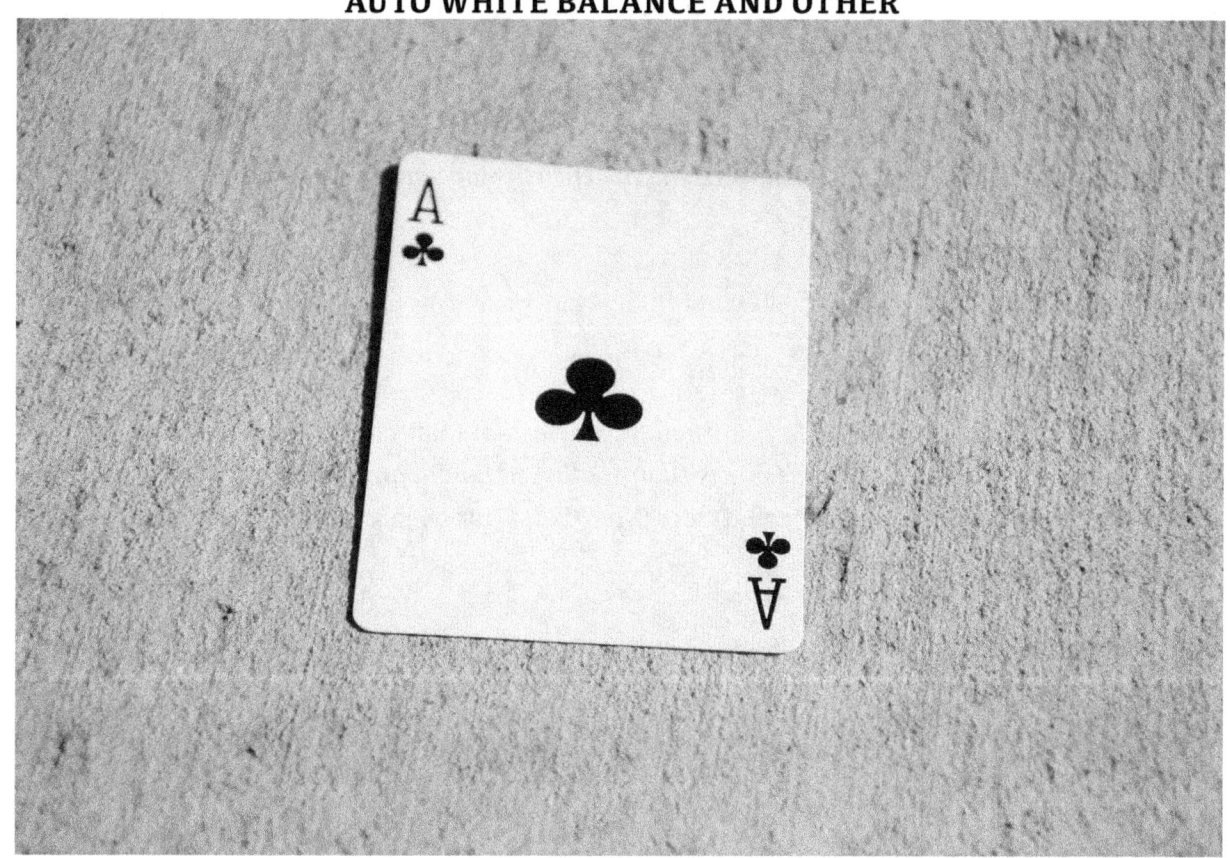

Auto White Balance

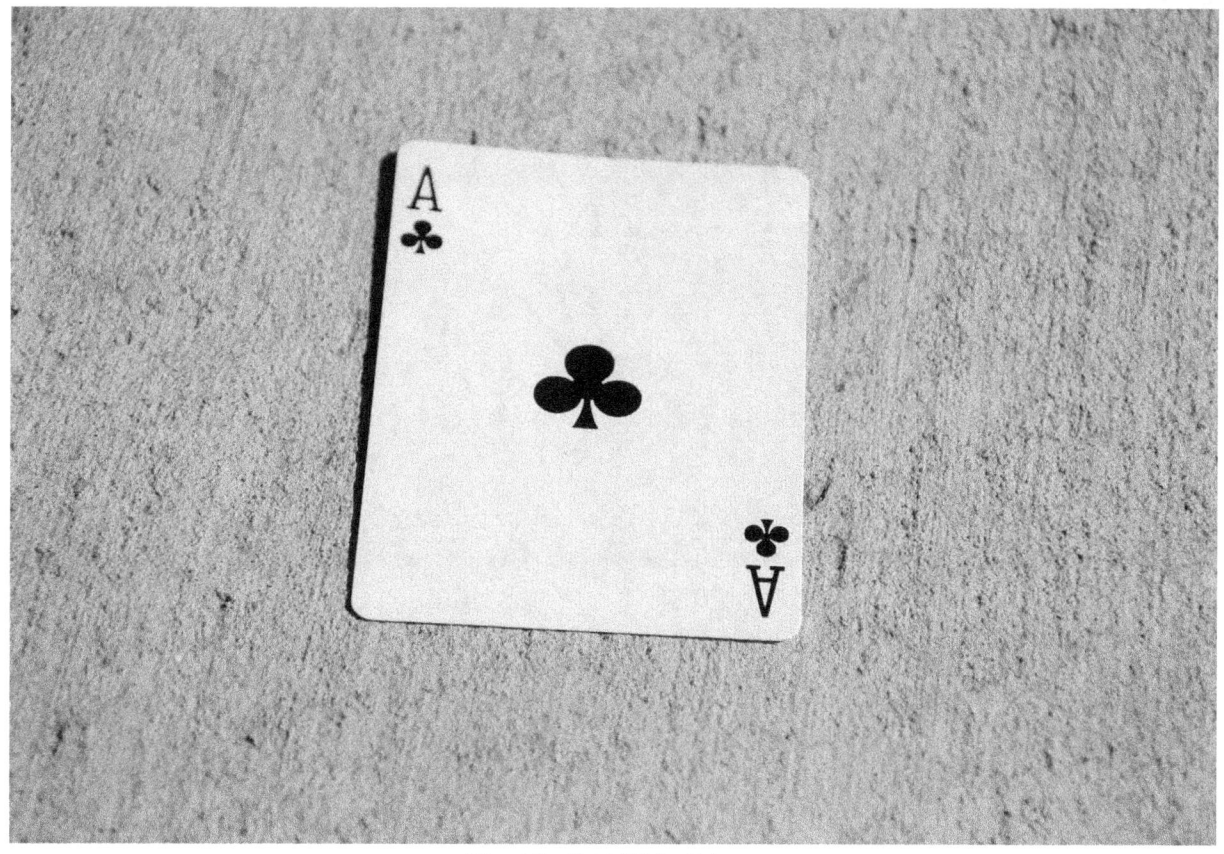

Direct Sunlight White Balance

OVERVIEW

The lighting condition used for all images is direct sun light.

Incandescent
When the white balance is set to Incandescent the entire image has a blue hue.

Cool-white fluorescent
When the white balance is set to Cool-white fluorescent the entire image has a lavender hue.

Flash
When the white balance is set to flash (although the flash did not go off) the image looks similar to the sunlight white balance image but is slightly darker. In Programed Mode the flash needs to be manually engaged on the Nikon d7100. Note: I did not engage the flash.

Cloudy
When the white balance is set to cloudy the entire image has a slight red hue. The red hue is mostly translucent.

Shade
When the white balance is set to shade the entire image has a sepia hue.

Conclusion
The greatest change in image color is with the white balance settings of Incandescent, Cool-white fluorescent, and shade. The former two are more of a problem than the latter two.

WHITE BALANCE ASSIGNMENT

Tools needed:
- Any subject or object
- Yellow highlighter
- Camera
- Tripod
- User guide

Things to Note

White Balance is set based on the source of the light you are photographing your subject in. That is, if you are in daylight and in the shade then you use the **shade** option or an equivalent based on your camera's user guide.

The next assignment will be done in one of the following lighting conditions: incandescent, fluorescent, direct sunlight, flash, cloudy, or shade. If your camera offers a light source not listed above and you have that light source available then feel free to use it.

STEPS for White Balance Assignment

1. **Document how to place your camera in Program Mode:**

2. **Document how to access your White Balance settings:**

3. **Document how to Manually Focus your Lens:**

4. Place camera on a **tripod** pointed toward desired subject/object.
5. Set Camera to **Programmed Mode**.
6. The lighting for your subject should be either incandescent, fluorescent, direct sunlight, flash, cloudy, or shade.
7. What lighting condition are you using? _____
8. Do not change the lighting conditions for the rest of this assignment.
9. **Manually** focus on a subject/object of your choice.
10. Snap a photo of your subject using **AUTO white balance**.
11. Snap a photo using the White Balance light setting you are using in **question 7**.
12. Snap a photo of the remaining white balance choices in step **#6**.
13. Return the white balance to **AUTO**.
14. Print, Cut, and Paste the **AUTO** white balanced image in the top box and the white balance image from **question 7** in the bottom box on the next page. Document the name of the white balance light source used for the bottom image.
15. **Overview**: Document your findings for step #12.

AUTO WHITE BALANCE AND OTHER

AUTO White Balance

White Balance type is?

OVERVIEW
The lighting condition used for all images is:

CUSTOM WHITE BALANCE

Generally you set your camera's white balance to the light source you are using. If you are indoors and the light source is an incandescent light then you set your camera's white balance to incandescent/indoors. If you are outside in direct sunlight then you set your camera's white balance to direct sunlight.

There are times when your subject will contain light from different sources as an indoor shot using incandescent lights and window light. On such occasions, of multiple light sources, you will need to use a custom (or manual) white balance.

Custom white balancing is done with a digital imaging gray card called a **white balance card**. On the computer the custom white balancing steps are as follows:
- Take a snapshot of the white balance card, it will serve as your reference image.
- Take the rest of your images in the same light situation.
- Download all images to your computer.
- Select the reference image (The image of the white balance card).
- Click on the white balance tool in your software to get a reading.
- Apply the reading numbers to the rest of your photos.

As one can see, the above method is software specific and hence not covered in this book. Our assignment will be done in camera.

CUSTOM WHITE BALANCE IN ACTION

Tools needed:
    Any Subject/Object
    Gray paper
    Camera
    Tripod
    User guide

Things to Note
The gray paper should be smooth, not rough.

STEPS for Custom White Balance in Action

1. Document how to place your camera in Program Mode:
On the Nikon D7100, press the <u>Mode dial lock release</u> button (top of camera) and rotate the mode dial to P. The P should be aligned to the white dot.

2. Document how to create/access your Custom White Balance settings:
Custom white balance with the Nikon d7100, by taking a <u>reference image</u> of a white or neutral gray sheet of paper.
- Place camera in Programmed mode.

In the below instructions, the camera is mapped to one of the 6 presets (d1-d6). After the newly created preset is selected the camera measures the value for the white balance then stores it in the newly created preset (d1-d6). In other words, you have to create a preset first, then store the white balance value into that preset. If the camera is able to get a measurement then the control panel will flash for about six seconds with the words Good or Gd. If the light is too dark and the camera is not able to get a white balance then the camera will display the words no Gd.

- Press <u>?/key WB</u> button.
- Rotate <u>Main Command dial</u> until PRE displays in the bottom right corner of control panel.
- Rotate <u>Sub-Command dial</u> for the desired preset (d-1 through d-6).
- Place a <u>neutral gray or white object</u> in the same lighting area as your photographs will be taken.
- Press <u>?/key WB</u> until the PRE icon starts flashing (PrE will appear in viewfinder). Before the flashing stops, <u>press the shutter button</u> to measure a value for white balance.
- Press <u>?/key WB</u> until the PRE icon starts flashing (PrE will appear in viewfinder). Go to desired preset.
- Snap the image with the newly measured preset.

3. Document how to place White Balance in Auto:
- Press <u>?/key WB</u> button.
- Rotate <u>Main Command dial</u> until the desired white balance option is AUTO.

4. Document how to Manually Focus your Lens:
On the Nikon D7100: Move the Focus-Mode selector to M. The Focus-Mode selector is on the front of the camera and has the letters AF and M stamped above it. To manually focus the lens, adjust the lens's focusing ring until the image is clear. The focusing ring is behind the zoom area of the lens.

5. Place camera on a **tripod** pointed toward desired subject/object.
6. Set Camera to **Programmed Mode**.
7. Do not change the lighting conditions for the rest of this assignment.
8. Take a **<u>reference image</u>** of a **light gray sheet of paper** (reference step #2).
9. **Manually** focus on a **subject/object** of **your choice**.
10. Snap a photo of your subject/object using your newly created white balance.
11. Snap a photo using the default Auto white balance.
12. Print, Cut, and Paste the custom white balanced image in the top box and the Auto white balance image in the bottom box on the next page.

WHITE BALANCE CUSTOM AND AUTO

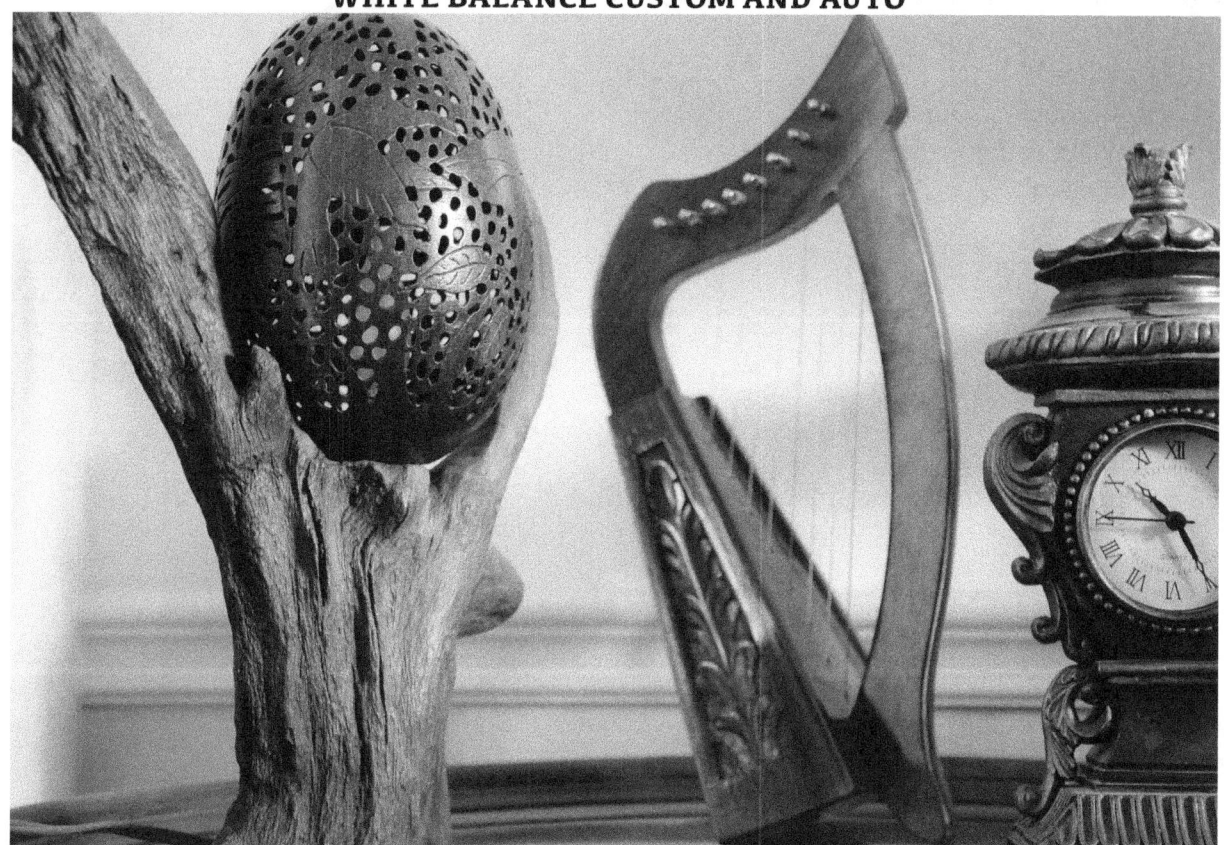

Custom White Balance

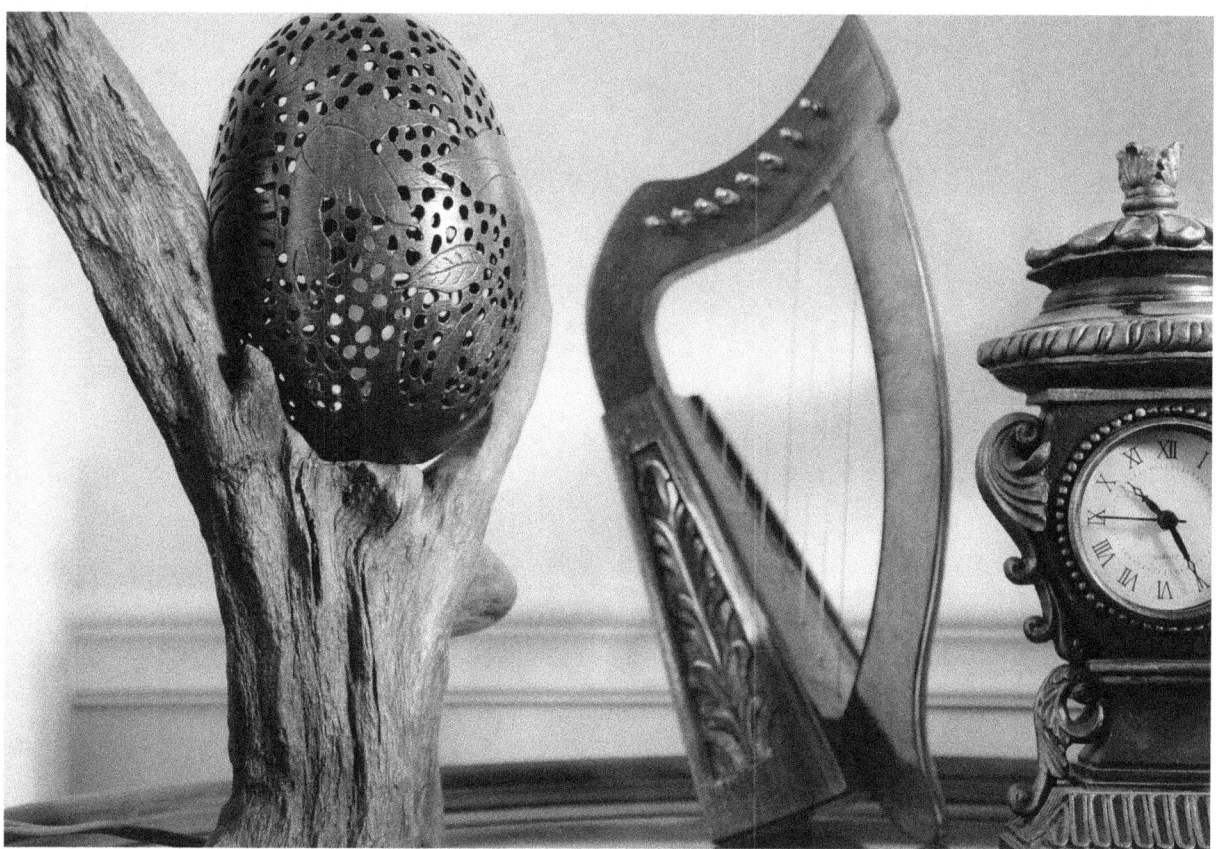

Auto White Balance

CUSTOM WHITE BALANCE ASSIGNMENT

Tools needed:
- Any Subject/Object
- White paper
- Camera
- Tripod
- User guide

Things to Note
The white paper should be smooth, not rough.

STEPS for Custom White Balance Assignment

1. **Document how to place your camera in Program Mode:**

2. **Document how to create/access your Custom White Balance settings:**

3. **Document how to place White Balance in Auto:**

4. **Document how to Manually Focus your Lens:**

5. Place camera on a **tripod** pointed toward desired subject/object.
6. Set Camera to **Programmed Mode**.
7. Do not change the lighting conditions for the rest of this assignment.
8. Take a <u>**reference image**</u> of a **white sheet of paper** (reference step #2).
9. **Manually** focus on a **subject/object** of **your choice**.
10. Snap a photo of your subject/object using your newly created white balance.
11. Snap a photo using the default Auto white balance.
12. Print, Cut, and Paste the custom white balanced image in the top box and the Auto white balance image in the bottom box on the next page.

WHITE BALANCE CUSTOM AND AUTO

Custom White Balance

Auto White Balance

MANUAL MODE

Manual exposure is the **M** in our acronym **MAPS**. With manual exposure the photographer controls the aperture and shutter speed.

When shooting in manual mode you need to first prioritize. Do you want, for example, a shallow depth of field? If yes then your priority is aperture settings. Do you want the action frozen in time? If yes then your priority is shutter speed. Is the representation of light the most important thing? If yes then your priority is ISO.

Once you decide on what is important to you then the next step is to set your other settings. Your camera will let you know if the exposure is correct by providing a small meter (exposure indicator) that will show whether the image will be underexposed or overexposed with the photographer's settings. Your goal as a photographer is to get the pointer in the middle at zero. That is, **to create a manual exposure**, set the aperture, then adjust the shutter speed until the meter moves to zero. Likewise, set the shutter speed, then adjust the aperture until the meter moves to zero.

$$\underline{-5\_\_\_4\_\_\_3\_\_\_2\_\_\_1\_\_\_\boxed{0}\_\_\_1\_\_\_2\_\_\_3\_\_\_4\_\_\_5}$$

Underexposed   Overexposed

Exposure Meter

Manual adjustment steps
    Set Aperture
    Adjust Shutter Speed until Meter moves to zero.

or

    Set Shutter Speed
    Adjust Aperture until Meter moves to zero.

MANUAL MODE IN ACTION

Tools needed:
    Any location, subject, or object
    Camera
    User guide

Things to Note
Fast shutter speeds freeze the action.
Slow shutter speeds blur the action.
Wide Apertures (small f number) give a shallow depth of field.
Shallow Apertures (big f numbers) give a wide depth of field.

Once the meter moves to **ZERO** you have a **correct exposure**.

STEPS for Manual Mode in Action

1. **Document how to place your camera in Manual Mode:**

On the Nikon D7100, press the <u>Mode dial lock release</u> button (top of camera) and rotate the mode dial to M. The M should be aligned to the white dot.

2. **Document how to set the camera's aperture.**

On the Nikon D7100: Rotate the <u>Sub Command dial</u>, on the front of the camera.

3. **Document how to adjust the shutter speed.**

On the Nikon D7100: Rotate the <u>Main Command dial</u>, on the back of the camera.

4. Set your camera on **Manual** mode (M).
5. Focus/refocus on any subject or object.
6. Select a **Shutter Speed** of your choice.
7. Adjust the **Aperture** until the meter moves to **zero**.

8. What is your Shutter Speed? *1/60*
9. What is your Aperture? *F6.3*

10. Select an **Aperture** of your choice (different from step 7).
11. Adjust the **Shutter Speed** until the meter moves to **zero**.

12. What is your Aperture? *F5*
13. What is your Shutter Speed? *1/80*

MANUAL MODE ASSIGNMENT

Tools needed:
    Any location, subject, or object
    Camera
    User guide

Things to Note
Fast shutter speeds freeze the action.
Slow shutter speeds blur the action.
Wide Apertures (small f number) give a shallow depth of field.
Shallow Apertures (big f numbers) give a wide depth of field.

Once the meter moves to **ZERO** you have a **correct exposure**.

STEPS for Manual Mode Assignment
Note, do not use the same values as the previous "in action" assignment.

1. **Document how to place your camera in Manual Mode:**

2. **Document how to set the camera's aperture.**

3. **Document how to adjust the shutter speed.**

4. Set your camera on **Manual** mode (M).
5. Focus/refocus on any subject or object.
6. Select a **Shutter Speed** of your choice.
7. Adjust the **Aperture** until the meter moves to **zero**.

8. What is your Shutter Speed? ____
9. What is your Aperture? _____

10. Select an **Aperture** of your choice (different from step 7).
11. Adjust the **Shutter Speed** until the meter moves to **zero**.

12. What is your Aperture? _____
13. What is your Shutter Speed? ____

MANUAL MODE SPECIAL ASSIGNMENT

By now you should be able to work assignments without step by step instructions. In this assignment you will focus on any subject or object, (moving or stationary).

1. Set your camera on **Manual** mode (M).

2. Open lens to widest Aperture (smallest f number).
3. What is the Aperture value (f number)? _____
4. Adjust **Shutter Speed** until the meter moves to **zero**.
5. What is the Shutter Speed value? _____
6. Snap the image.

7. Stop down the Aperture by **one stop**.
8. What is the Aperture value (f number)? _____
9. Adjust the Shutter Speed until the meter moves to **zero**.
10. What is the Shutter Speed value? _____
11. Snap the image.
12. Continue the above process all the way to the narrowest aperture on your lens (biggest f number)
13. Document the **File name**, **f number**, **Exposure time**, **ISO**, and **Focal length**.
14. **Overview**: look at all your images and explain your findings, plus answer the two questions in the overview section.

File name	F-Number	Exposure Time (Shutter Speed)	ISO	Focal Length

OVERVIEW
- Is the shutter speed changing by one stop or more than one stop?
- Exposure wise all of these images are the same. Do they look the same creatively?

LONG EXPOSURE

During our shutter speed chapter we learned that keeping the shutter opened too long when taking outdoor daytime shots produces an image overexposed. Even when the aperture was stepped down (lower f number) the image was still overexposed in daytime light. Hence, outdoor shots needed a faster shutter speed.

Slower shutter speeds can be used with night scenery and moving lights to produce a creative image. This scenario is often seen with moving headlights of cars. To produce such an exposure, the shutter speed is set to either **Bulb** or **Time**.

Bulb and Time
There are two special exposure modes you might encounter while shooting in **Manual mode**, namely, **Bulb** (buLb) and **Time** (- -). Bulb and Time are shutter speed settings that allow for a long exposure. In other words, the shutter is opened for a long time.

Bulb: the shutter stays open as long as the shutter release button is depressed.

Time (- -): the button is pressed to open the shutter then pressed again to close the shutter. The shutter may alternatively close at a predetermined time based on your camera's specs.

LONG EXPOSURE in Action

Tools needed:
- Any nigh time location
- Flash light
- Camera
- Tripod
- User guide

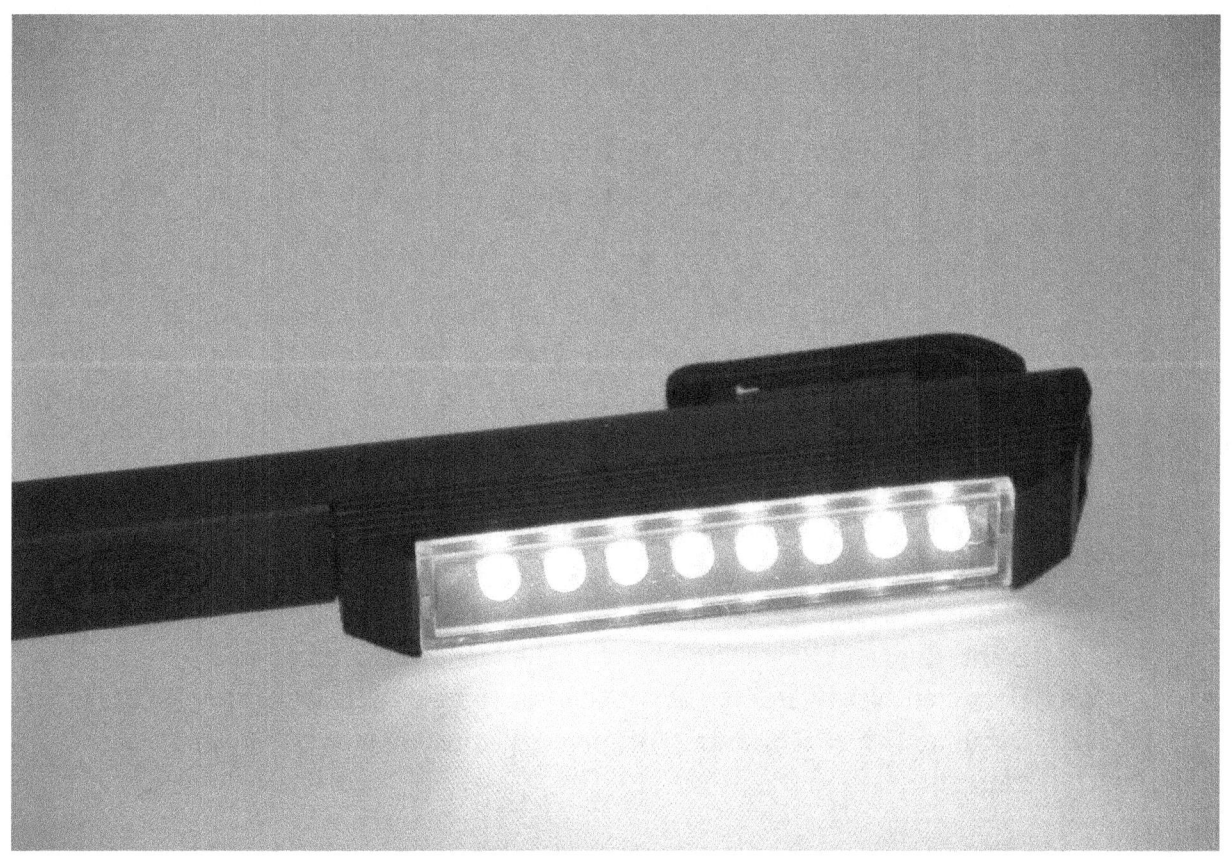

Flash light

ACCESSING IMAGE INFORMATION

This assignment will require accessing image information. To access the F number, Exposure time, ISO, and Focal Length, do the following:

- **MAC**: right click the file, select *Get Info*, then click the down arrow under *More Info*. You will need your camera's software to see the ISO settings on a MAC.
- **PC**: right click the file, select *Properties*, click the *Details* tab, scroll down to Camera.

Things to Note

We will do a long exposure in this section.

When we set the shutter speed to Bulb or Time we are opening the shutter.

This same project can be done at any nighttime location with moving lights (street scene with cars).

STEPS for Long Exposure in Action

1. Document how to place your camera in Manual Mode:

On the Nikon D7100, press the <u>Mode dial lock release</u> button (top of camera) and rotate the mode dial to M. The M should be aligned to the white dot.

2. Document how to set the camera's aperture.

On the Nikon D7100: Rotate the <u>Sub Command dial</u>, on the front of the camera, to the right to step down the aperture (bigger f numbers) and to the left to open up the aperture (smaller f numbers).

3. Document how to set the shutter speed to Bulb

On the Nikon D7100: Rotate the <u>Main Command dial</u>, on the back of the camera, to the left until Bulb is displayed.

4. Place camera on a **tripod** and zoom all the way out (wide angle).
5. Set your camera on **Manual mode (M)**.
6. Step down on the aperture to it's lowest f number. What is the f number? *f22*
7. Set the shutter speed to **Bulb**.
8. Press the shutter release button and keep it pressed down.
9. Move a flash light in front of the camera lens for about **15 seconds**.
10. Release the shutter release button.
11. Print, Cut, and Paste the image in the box on the next page.
12. Document your findings about the image below the image.
13. Document the **File name**, **F number**, **Exposure time**, **ISO**, and **Focal Length**.

BULB SHUTTER SPEED

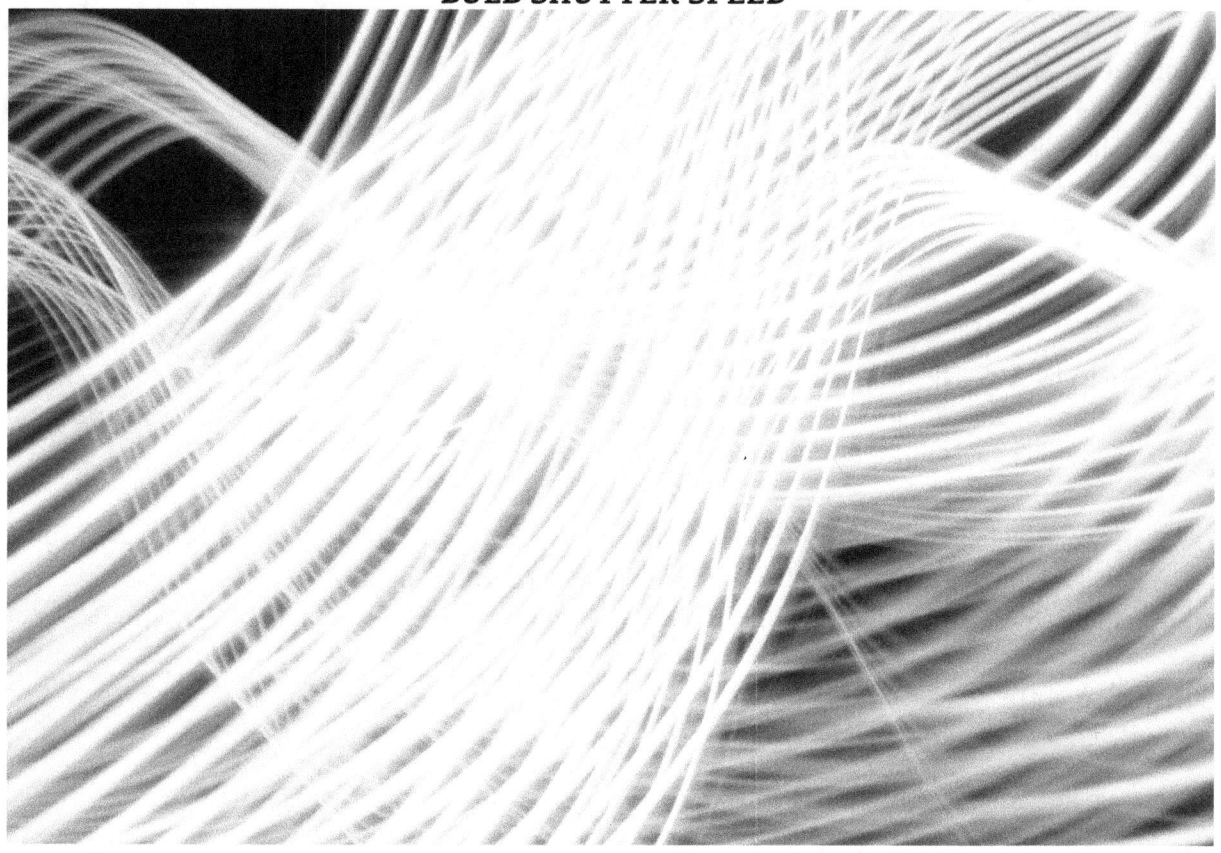

Long Exposure using BULB

IMAGE INFORMATION

File name	F-Number	Exposure Time (Shutter Speed)	ISO	Focal Length
DSC_0625.jpg	f22	14.8s	100	22mm

LONG EXPOSURE Assignment

Tools needed:
- Any nigh time location
- Flash light
- Camera
- Tripod
- User guide

ACCESSING IMAGE INFORMATION

This assignment will require accessing image information. To access the F number, Exposure time, ISO, and Focal Length, do the following:

- **MAC**: right click the file, select *Get Info*, then click the down arrow under *More Info*. You will need your camera's software to see the ISO settings on a MAC.
- **PC**: right click the file, select *Properties*, click the *Details* tab, scroll down to Camera.

Things to Note

We will do a long exposure in this section.

When we set the shutter speed to Bulb or Time we are opening the shutter.

This same project can be done at any nighttime location with moving lights (street scene with cars.)

STEPS for Long Exposure Assignment

1. **Document how to place your camera in Manual Mode:**

2. **Document how to set the camera's aperture.**

3. **Document how to set the shutter speed to Time (--)**

4. Place camera on a **tripod** and zoom all the way out (wide angle).
5. Set your camera on **Manual mode (M)**.
6. Step down on the aperture to it's lowest f number. What is the f number? ___
7. Set the shutter speed to **Time (--)**.
8. Press the shutter release button.
9. Walk in front of the camera moving the flash light about your body.
10. After **30 seconds** press the shutter release button again.
11. Print, Cut, and Paste the image in the box on the next page.
12. Document your findings about the image below the image.
13. Document the **File name, F number, Exposure time, ISO**, and **Focal Length**.

TIME (- -) SHUTTER SPEED

IMAGE INFORMATION

File name	F-Number	Exposure Time (Shutter Speed)	ISO	Focal Length

ASPECT RATIO

The **aspect ratio** of an image is the relationship between the width of the image and the height of the image. Aspect ratio is written as **width:height** where the width will always come first. Generally you will need to select the aspect ratio for the images you desire to capture.

The following is a list of aspect ratios you as a photographer might encounter.
- **3:2** Suitable for standard prints (same proportions as a frame of 35mm film.)
- **4:3** Good for viewing on a Computer.
- **4:3** VGA good for email attachments.
- **16:9** Good for viewing on High Definition (HD) devices (wide TV).
- **1:1** Pictures are square.

The number to the left of the colon is the width. The number to the right of the colon is the height. Please note that the aspect ratio is not a specific number but a relationship between two numbers.

Just understand that the actual size of the image in pixels may be different from camera to camera yet the aspect ratio may be the same.

Take, for example, a 3:2 aspect ratio. Any of the following dimensions will produce a 3:2 aspect ratio: 300 x 200, 600 x 400, 1200 x 800, 1350 x 900, 2700 x 1800, and 6000 x 4000. That is, taking 300 x 200 and dividing each by 100 yields 3 x 2 which is a 3:2 ratio. Likewise, taking 6000 x 4000 and dividing each by 2000 yields 3 x 2, which again is a 3:2 ratio.

Now, let's explore a 4:3 aspect ratio. Any of the following dimensions will produce a 4:3 aspect ratio: 400 x 300, 800 x 600, 1280 x 960, 1600 x 1200, 1800 x 1350, 2592 x 1944, 3600 x 2700, 3648 x 2736. That is, taking 400 x 300 and dividing each by 100 yields 4 x 3 which is a 4:3 ratio.

The dimensions you set your camera to photograph images at is extremely important due to standard printing options. Most printing options are as follows:

Print Size	Aspect Ratio
4 x 6	3:2
5 x 7	7:5
8 x 10	5:4

Aspect Ratio

When you print with a different aspect ratio than what your images were taken as, you end up having to crop out part of your images. **Crop** means to remove. The best thing to do is to set your aspect ratio to the aspect that you usually print in. If you normally print 4 x 6 images then an aspect ratio of 3:2 is desirable. If you normally print 8 x 10 then the 5:4 aspect ratio is desirable. The only other desirable option is the crop your images before sending them to be commercially printed, otherwise the printer will determine what to crop.

An aspect ratio of 3:2 can be a 4 x 6 print, or an 8 x 12 print. We obtain 8 x 12 from multiplying the height and width of the 4 x 6 print by 2.
    4 X 2 = 8
    6 X 2 = 12

An aspect ratio of 5:4 can be an 8 x 10 print or a 4 x 5 print. We obtain 4 x 5 from dividing the height and width of the 8 x 10 print by 2.
    8/2 = 4
    10/2 = 5

It is best to think of ratios in terms of multiplication factors.
    A **3:2** ratio means the short side times **1.5** is the value of the long side.
    A **5:7** ratio means the short side times **1.4** is the value of the long side.
    A **5:4** ratio means the short side times **1.25** is the value of the long side.

Using the multiplication factors (1.5, 1.4, and 1.25) we can set three images at an **equal height** of 4 (**4H**) and still maintain our aspect ratios with different widths (**W**).

3:2 ratio: 4x6 image, 4H x 1.5 = 6W.   Hence we maintain a 4 x 6 image.
5:7 ratio: 5x7 image, 4H x 1.4 = 5.6W.   Hence we have a smaller 4 x 5.6 image.
5:4 ratio: 8x10 image, 4H x 1.25 = 5W.   Hence we have a smaller 4 x 5 image.

By keeping a constant height, the 8 x 10 image has shrunk to 4 x 5, and the 5 x 7 image has shrunk to 4 x 5.6. Both the 8 x 10 and the 5 x 7 image are now smaller than the 4 x 6 image (See photo below).

Aspect Ratio size Comparison

When printing a 4 x 6 image using the 3:2 aspect ratio, the entire image is in the frame.

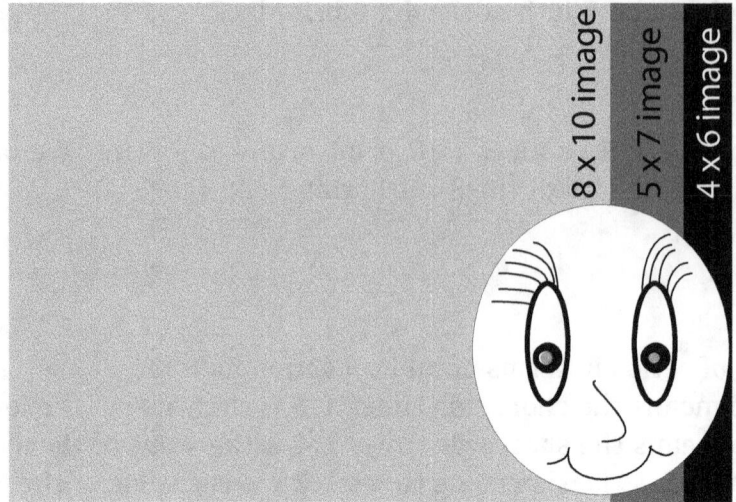

Aspect Ratio 3:2 with a 4x6 print

When printing a 5x7 image using the 3:2 aspect ratio, part of the face is chopped off.

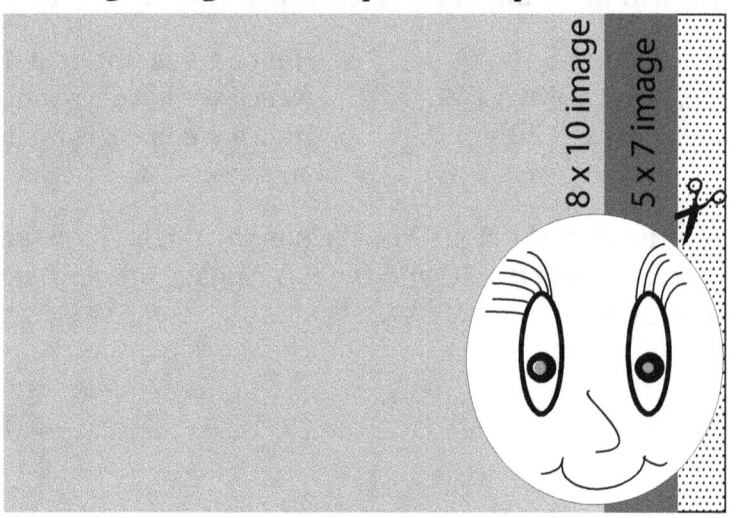

Aspect Ratio 7:5 with a 5x7 print

When printing an 8x10 image using the 3:2 aspect ratio, half of the face is chopped off.

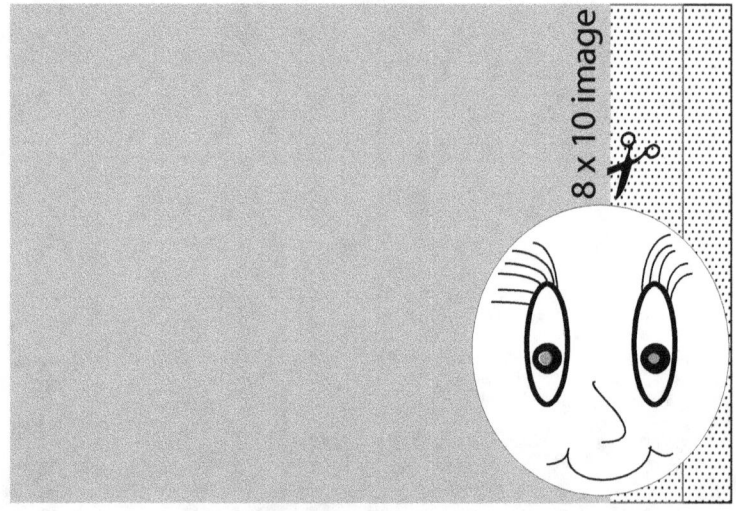

Aspect Ration 5:4 with an 8x10 print

Look at the following image. Note how part of the building will be chopped off if the image is printed in a size other than 4 x 6. Which part will the printer crop off?

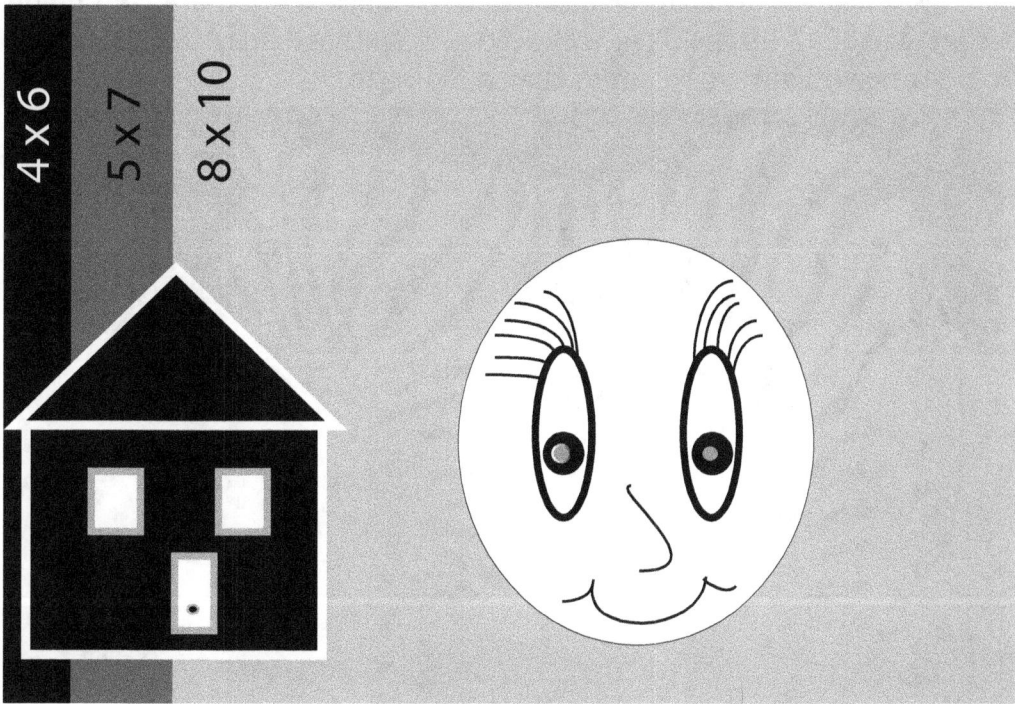

Image needing a crop

To avoid loosing critical parts of your image, it is recommended to crop your images before sending them to the printer. I cropped the right side from the image below to remove the unneeded blank space. Now the person and the house remain in the image.

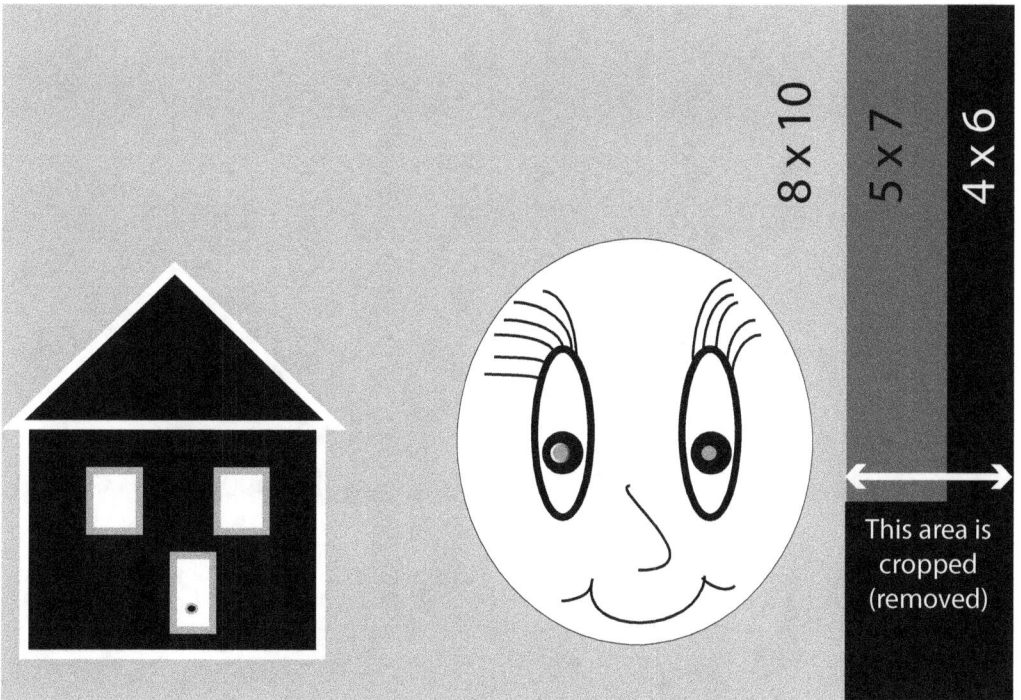

Image crop area selected by photographer

Ideally, the photographer should take images in the correct aspect format. Most consumers print in 4x6 (3:2 aspect ratio).

3:2 ratio vs 5:4 ratio
If your camera is set to a 3:2 aspect ratio, you can easily print an 8 x 12 image. The problem arises when you want to print an 8 x 10 image, as you are **two inches short** (10 inches instead of 12 inches). You will need to crop those extra two inches from your image. A 3:2 ratio will always be larger than a 5:4 ratio.

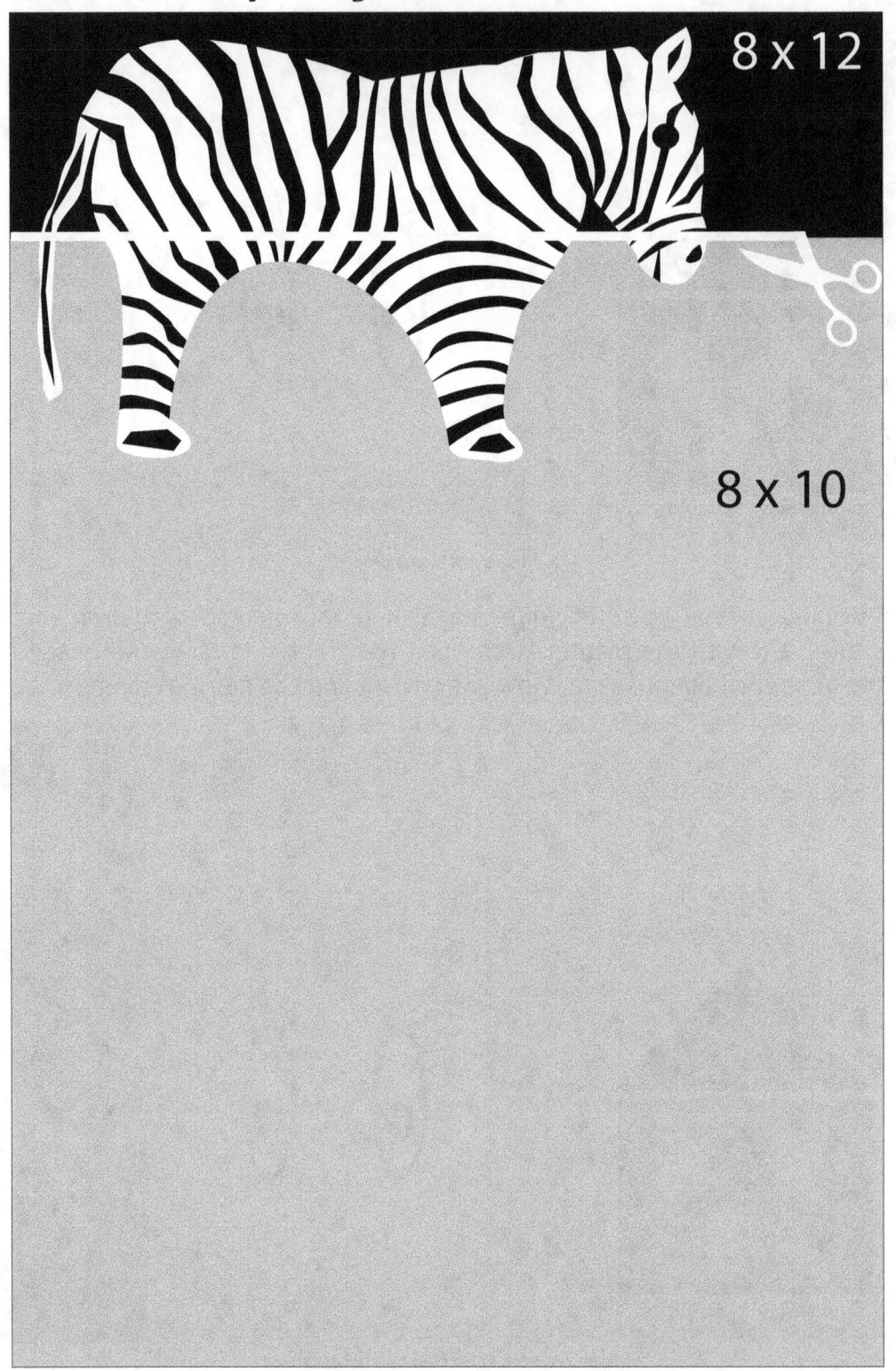

Two inch crop

The 8 x 10 is derived from our **4 x 5**, where each side is multiplied by two.

3:2 ratio vs 5:7 ratio

If your camera is set to a 3:2 aspect ratio, you can easily print an 8 x 12 image. The problem arises when you want to print an 8 x 11.2 image, as you are **.8 inches short** (11.2 inches instead of 12 inches). You will need to crop those extra .8 inches from your image. A 3:2 ratio will always be larger than a 5:7 ratio.

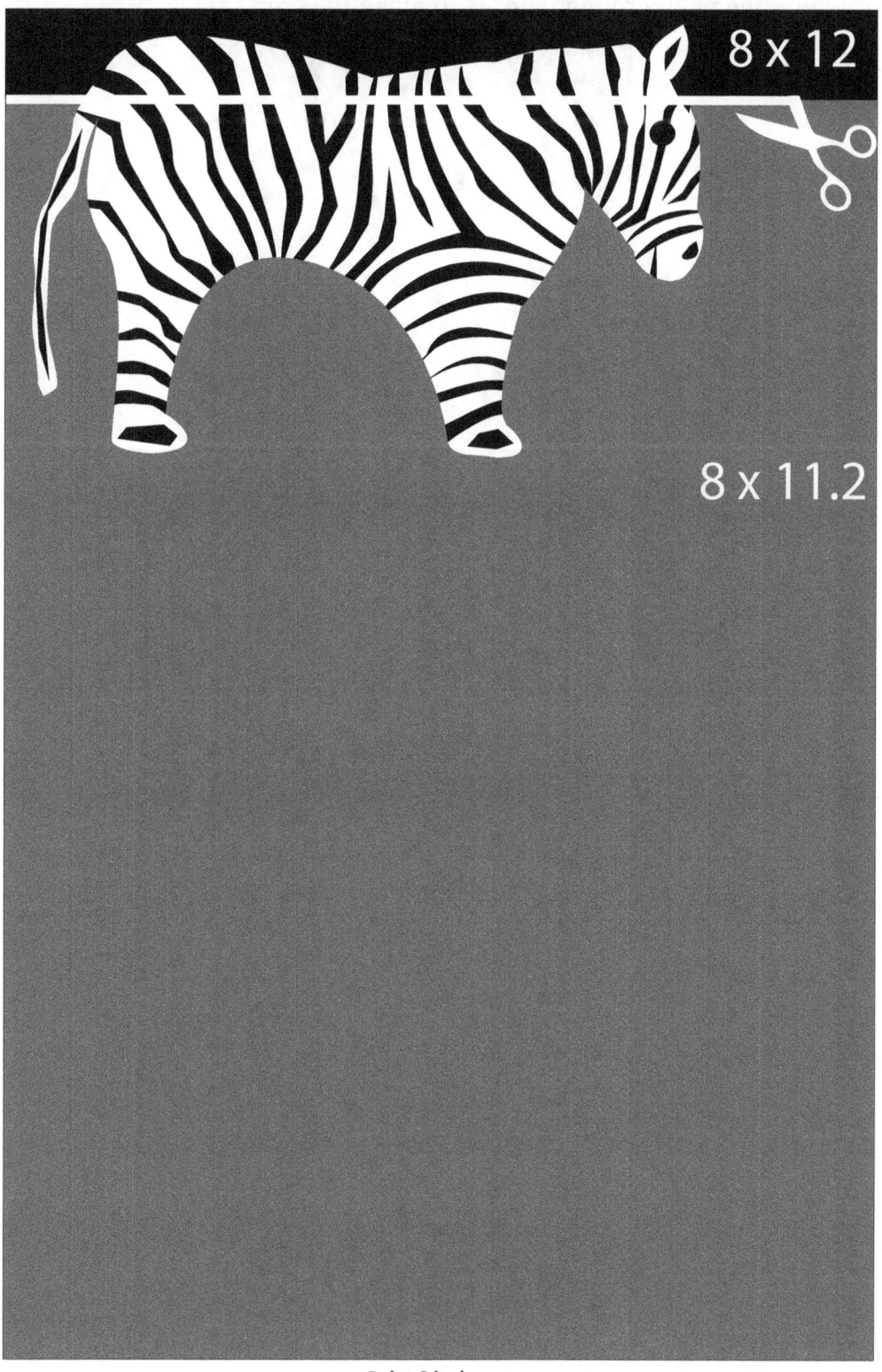

Point 8 inch crop

The 8 x 11.2 is derived from our **4 x 5.6**, where each side is multiplied by two.

When printing in the wrong aspect ratio, the photographer has three choices: **Crop to size**, **Stretch to fit**, or **Fit in frame**.

CROP TO SIZE
Crop to size is what we have studied so far. The two images below are exactly the same except for where the photographer choses to make the crop.

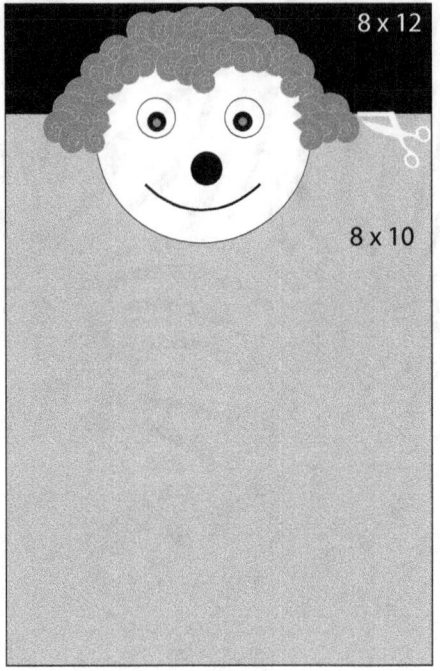

(A) Crop to Size

If the image above is cropped at the top, part of the person's face will be chopped off.

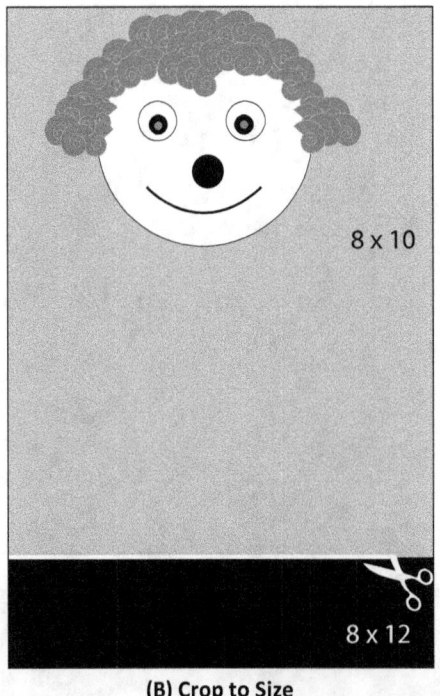

(B) Crop to Size

This bottom image is cropped at the bottom to preserve our subject. Option B is more desirable than option A unless you specifically want someone removed from a photo.

STRETCH TO FIT

We can stretch our 8 x 12 image to make it fit into an 8 x 10 frame. Stretching the image causes **distortion**. Note how the face (plus eyes and nose) in A, B, and D, is perfectly ROUND. The circular objects in C are more OVAL in shape. This is due to distortion.

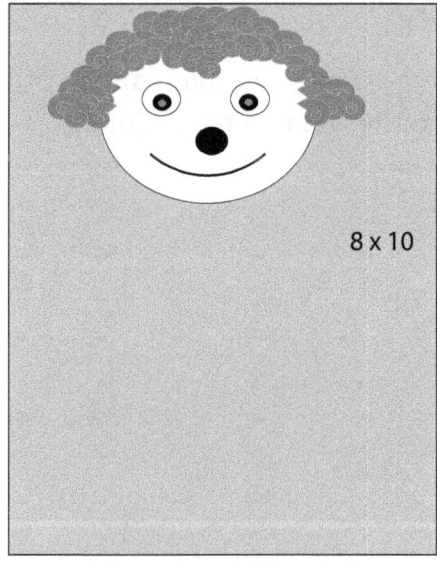

(C) Stretch to Fit (distorted)

FIT IN FRAME

Fit in frame allows us to get the entire photo to fit proportionally in the frame (no distortion) without having to crop our image. The trade-off for this convenience is that we get white borders around the image.

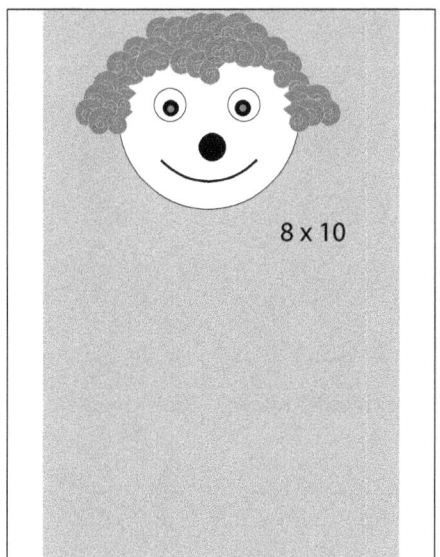

(D) Fit in Frame (white borders))

Which is better? It depends on what you, the photographer, desire.

ASPECT RATIO ASSIGNMENT

Tools Needed
    User guide

1. How many aspect ratios does your camera offer?
2. List the aspect ratios your camera offers.
3. What aspect ratio will you use the most? _____

SENSOR SIZE

A photograph is made of light. Everything we have studied so far has been in terms of light. The sensor is no different. The larger the sensor then the more light your camera can capture.

The size of 35mm film is about 36 mm x 24 mm. In the digital world this is known as a Full Frame sensor and is our base point for determining sensor size. Most full frame digital cameras are extremely expensive hence many consumers and enthusiasts opt for the lower priced APS-C sensors. As a general rule, the larger the sensor the better the image quality. In practicality, there are more aspects determining image quality than just a sensor size.

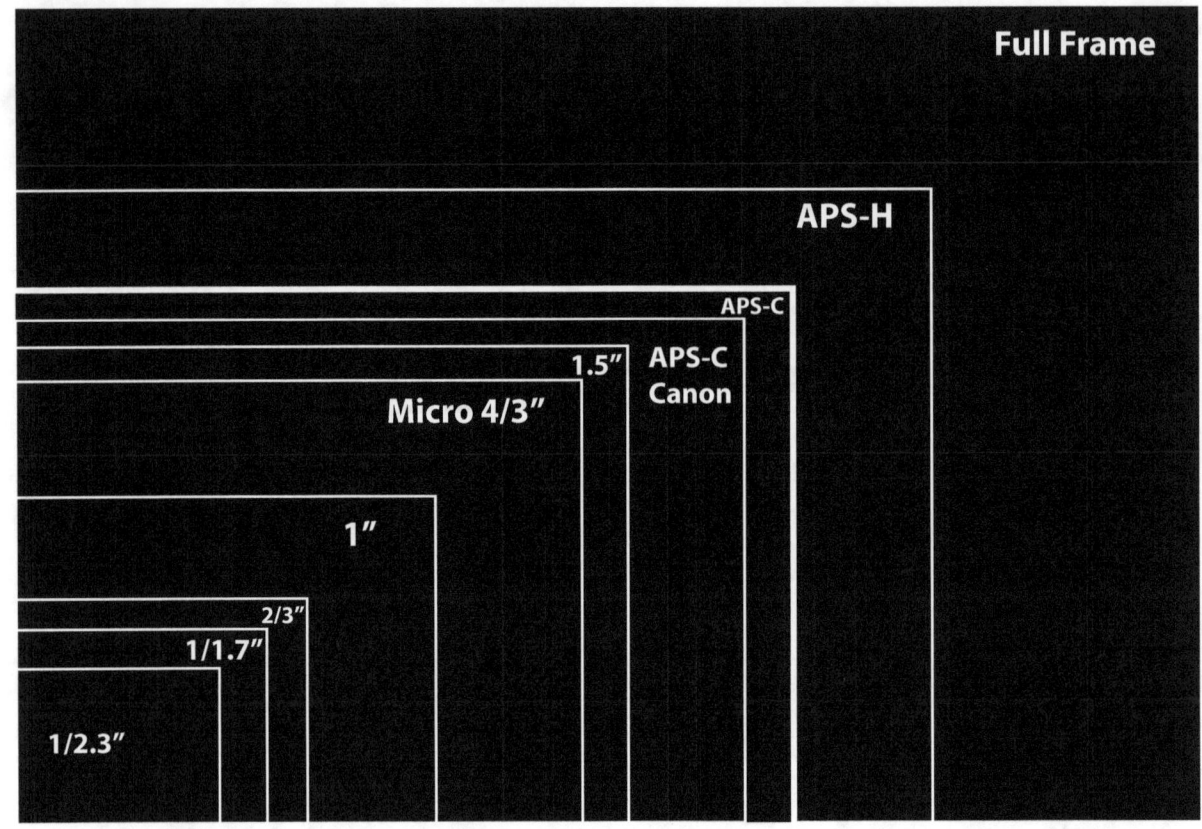

Sensor Sizes

Sensor Type	Millimeters	Sample Camera Models
Full Frame	36 x 24	Sony RX 1, Nikon d800
APS-H	27.9 x 18.6	Canon 1D Mark IV
APS-C	23.6 x 15.6	Nikon d7100
APS-C (Canon)	22.2 x 14.8	Canon EOS 600D
1.5"	18.7 x 14	Canon G1
Micro Four Thirds (4/3)	17.3 x 13	Olympus Pen E-PL5
1"	12.8 x 9.6	Sony RX100
2/3"	8.8 x 6.6	Fujifilm FinePix X20
1/1.7"	7.6 x 5.7	Casio EX-Z1200
1/2.3"	6.17 x 4.55	Pentax Q

Sensor Size Camera Examples

All focal lengths in this book are listed in terms of a Nikon D7100 crop factor which is about 1.5. This means that for any given lens used on the D7100, the focal length needs to be multiplied by 1.5 to show the equivalent area on a full frame 35mm digital single lens reflex camera (dSLR). If I use a 300mm focal length on the d7100, then in the full frame world, to see the exact same area, I need an equivalent focal length of 450mm. On the flip side, if I was using a full frame camera and zoomed in to 450mm, I would be able to see that same area on an APS-C (Nikon d7100) sensor using only a 300mm zoom lens.

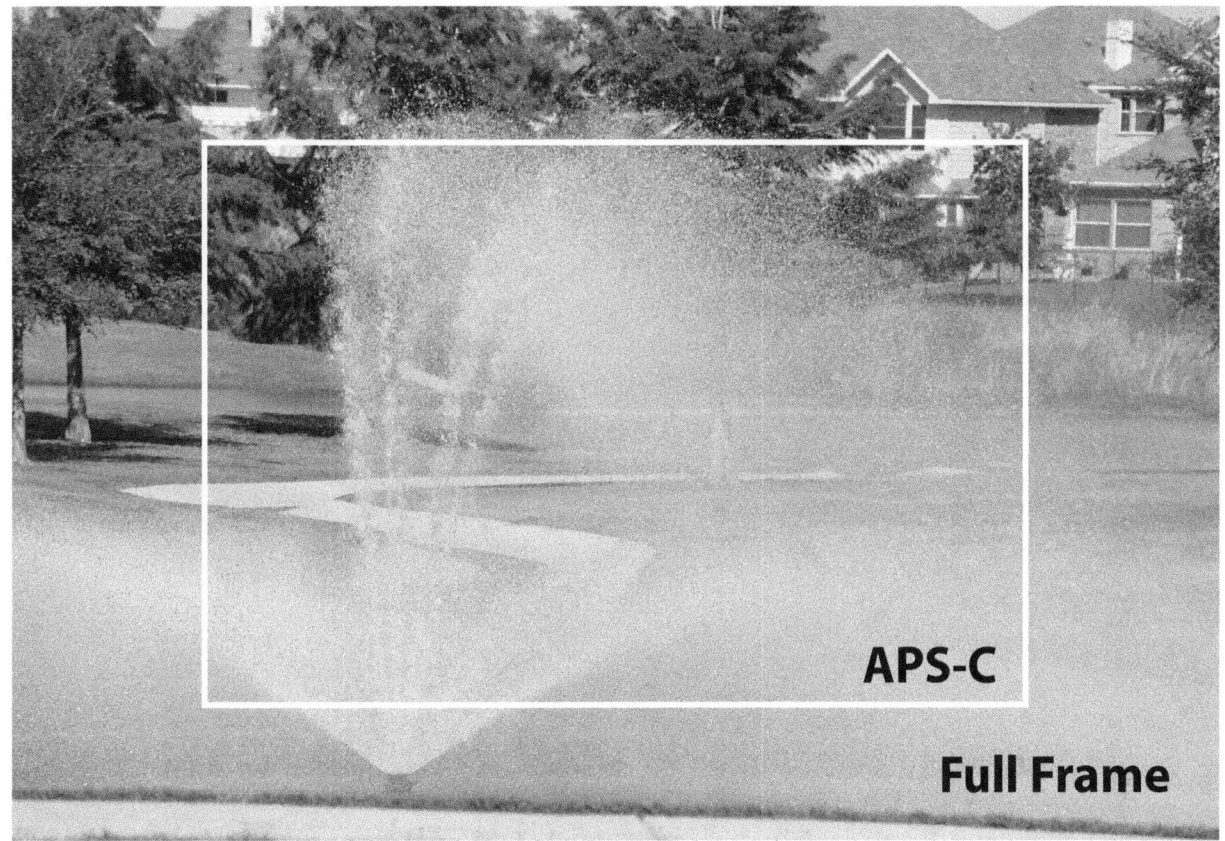

Crop Factor

If the image above was taken with a full frame camera at 20 mm then you would see the entire image (full frame). On an APS-C camera, you would only see the center frame which would be equivalent to a 30 mm zoom on the full frame camera. That is, take 20 mm times 1.5 (the crop factor) and you get 30 mm. It should be noted that the smaller the sensor size then the more of a crop factor you will obtain. The **Sony RX100** has about a 2.7 crop factor.

Notes:
4 x 6, Full Frame image.
1.5, Crop Factor.
4 divided by 1.5 = 2.67
6 divided by 1.5 = 4
2.67 x 4, APS-C image all encapsulated into a 4 x 6 frame.

SENSOR SIZE ASSIGNMENT

    1.   Document the size of your camera's sensor.

You may need to search the web to find this information. Be sure to include the name and model number of your camera. For example, Nikon d7100, sensor size APS-C.

LIGHT

We have learned a lot in the previous chapters. The information we have learned all have a common theme, LIGHT. Aperture priority either stopped down the light or stepped up the light. Shutter speed priority either stopped down the light or stepped up the light. ISO stopped down the light or stepped up the light. Exposure Compensation either stopped down the light or stepped up the light. Ditto for Bracketing and Manual mode. The histogram and white balance is affected by light. Even sensor size has a direct correlation to the light entering the camera. Photography is about light, light, and more light. Generally you will work with the doubling and halving of light.

A photograph is light, light, and more light

Provided the ISO is constant, when we adjust our aperture we can also adjust our shutter speed to maintain a correct exposure.

Suppose we have a correct exposure at aperture f8, ISO 100, and a shutter speed of 1/125 (see image below). If we step down our aperture to f11 then we can keep the correct exposure by decreasing the speed of the shutter to 1/60. If we stop down to f16 then we need to change the shutter to a slower speed of 1/30 to allow more light to enter the camera.

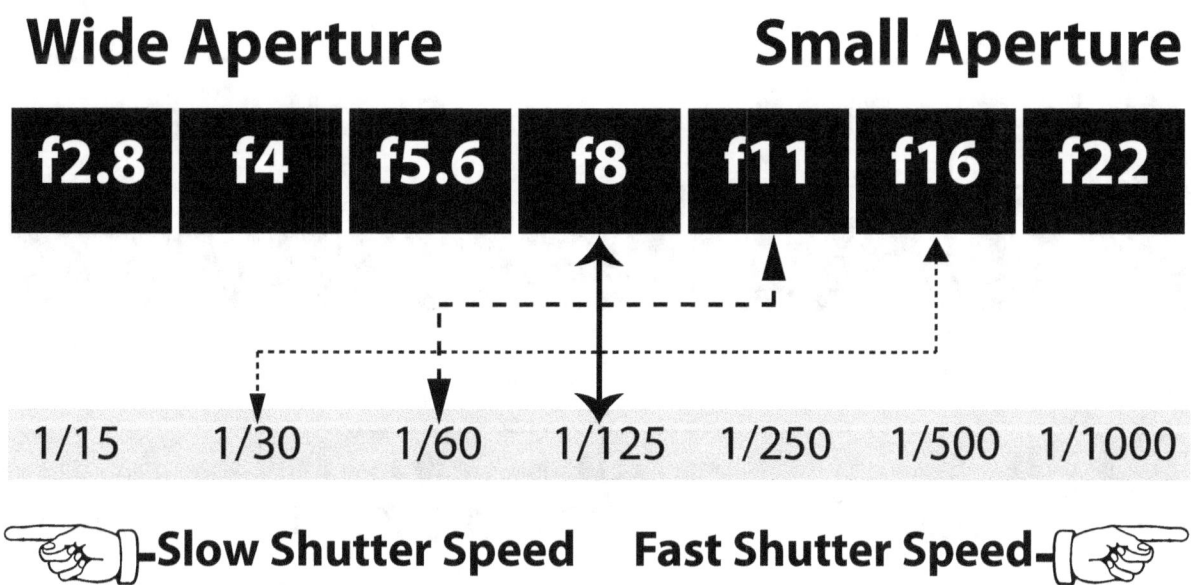

Aperture and Shutter Speed Illustration 1

Remember that when we decrease (or slow down) the **speed** of the shutter's opening and closing, it is also called increasing the shutter as we are increasing the **time** the shutter stays open. Below are the possible scenarios of shutter speed lingo. Each scenario can possibly be on opposite ends of the chart.

Increase the shutter can mean:
Increase the TIME the shutter stays open (Slower Shutter Speeds).
Increase the SPEED in which the shutter opens and closes (Faster Shutter Speeds).
Decrease the TIME the shutter stays open (Faster Shutter Speeds).

Decrease the shutter can mean:
Decrease the TIME the shutter stays open (Faster Shutter Speeds).
Decrease the SPEED in which the shutter opens and closes (Slower Shutter Speeds).
Increase the TIME the shutter stays open (Slower Shutter Speeds).

This book will normally refer to SPEED as opposed to TIME when referring to shutter speeds. Thus if a shutter speed is said to increase then it means the shutter opens and closes faster. If the shutter speed is said to decrease then it means the shutter opens and closes slower. Hence, a shutter speed increase is a faster shutter speed (from 1/500 to 1/1000); a shutter speed decrease is a slower shutter speed. The main thing is to know what shutter speed lingo a person is speaking in.

Suppose we have a correct exposure at aperture f8, ISO 100, and a shutter speed of 1/125 (see image below). If we step up our aperture to f5.6 then we can keep the correct exposure by increasing the speed of the shutter to 1/250. If we stop up to f4 then we need to change the shutter to a faster speed of 1/500 to allow less light to enter the camera. Remember that when we increase (or speed up) the **speed** of the shutter's opening and closing, it is also called decreasing the shutter as we are decreasing the **time** the shutter stays open.

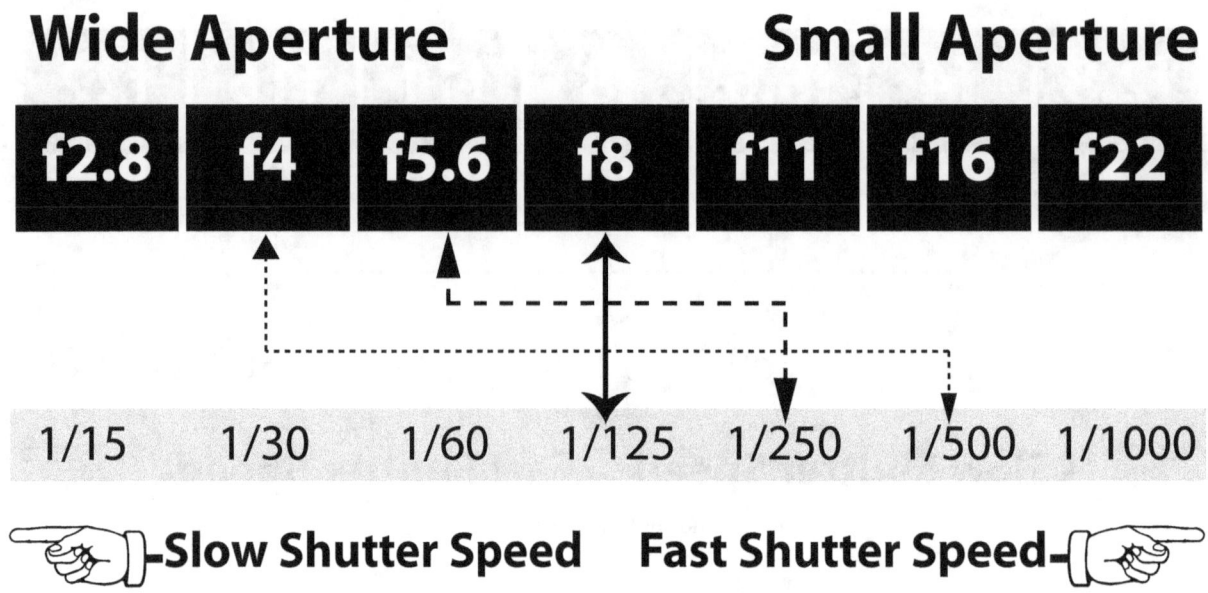

Aperture and Shutter Speed Illustration 2

Note that the numbers above are based on f8 at 1/125 being the correct exposure. If some other value is the correct exposure then the shutter speed and aperture will shift accordingly.

The essence of the charts above were done is to maintain equality. As we move to the right on one chart we move to the left on the other chart. Likewise, as we move to the left on one chart then we move to the right on another chart.

If we rewrite how the chart above is laid out then we get the chart below. We simply maintain equality by increasing (making faster) the shutter speed when the aperture is wide (small number), and decreasing (making slower) the shutter speed when the aperture is small (big number). That is, if we stop down our aperture to f11 then we must change our shutter speed to 1/60 to keep the correct exposure. If we change our shutter speed to 1/1000 then we must step up the aperture to f2.8 to maintain the correct exposure.

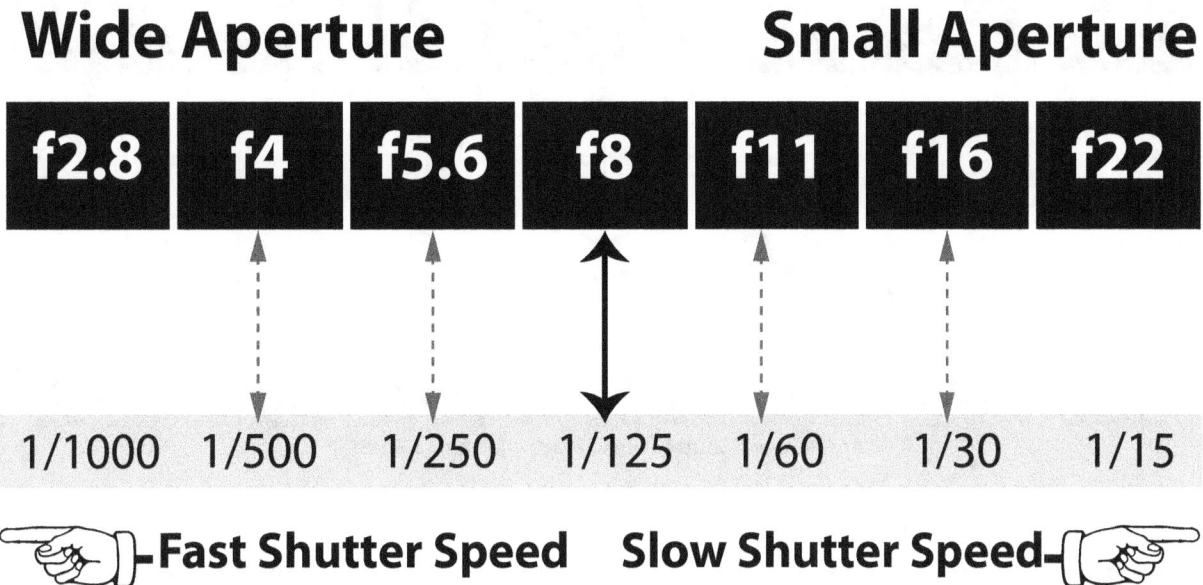

Aperture and Shutter Speed Illustration 3

Our chart is based on the correct exposure at aperture f8, ISO 100, and a shutter speed of 1/125. What if we increase the ISO from 100 to 200? What happens to the shutter speed?

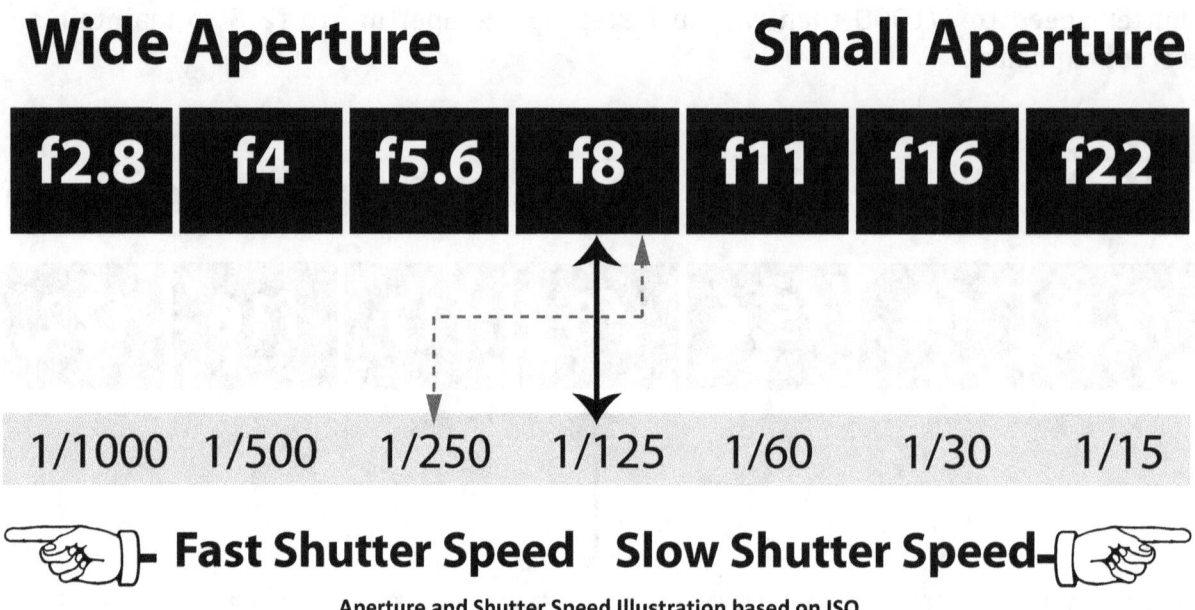

Aperture and Shutter Speed Illustration based on ISO

If we increase the ISO from 100 to 200, we are increasing it's light sensitivity by one stop. Therefore we must decrease the light that the shutter speed allows into the camera by one stop. Hence we would change our shutter speed from 1/125 to 1/250 to maintain a correct exposure. Alternatively, we can keep the same shutter speed of 1/125 and step down the aperture from f8 to f11.

Remember, the stopping down of the aperture (by one stop) means cutting the LIGHT in half. Stepping up the aperture by one stop doubles the LIGHT. Decreasing the speed of the shutter (increasing how long the shutter stays open) gives an extra stop of LIGHT (doubles the light). Increasing the speed of the shutter (decreasing how long the shutter stays open) halves the LIGHT. It is ALL about LIGHT.

Aperture

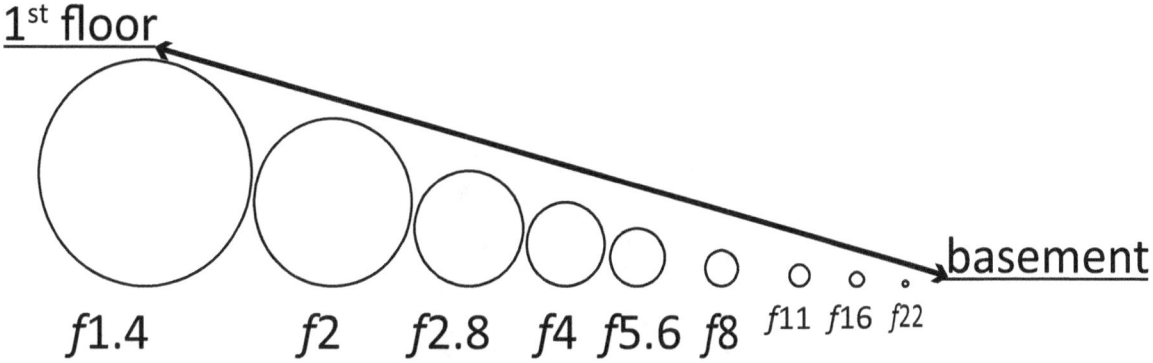

Shutter Speed

Aperture and Shutter Speed

With a wider aperture (small f number) we open and close the shutter quickly. With a smaller aperture (big f number) we open and close the shutter slowly.

Why is this light so important?
If we have too much light the image is overexposed. If we have too little light the image is underexposed. In essence, exposure is a measurement of light. We control the light for exposure with aperture, shutter speed, and ISO. Those three variables make up the Exposure Pyramid.

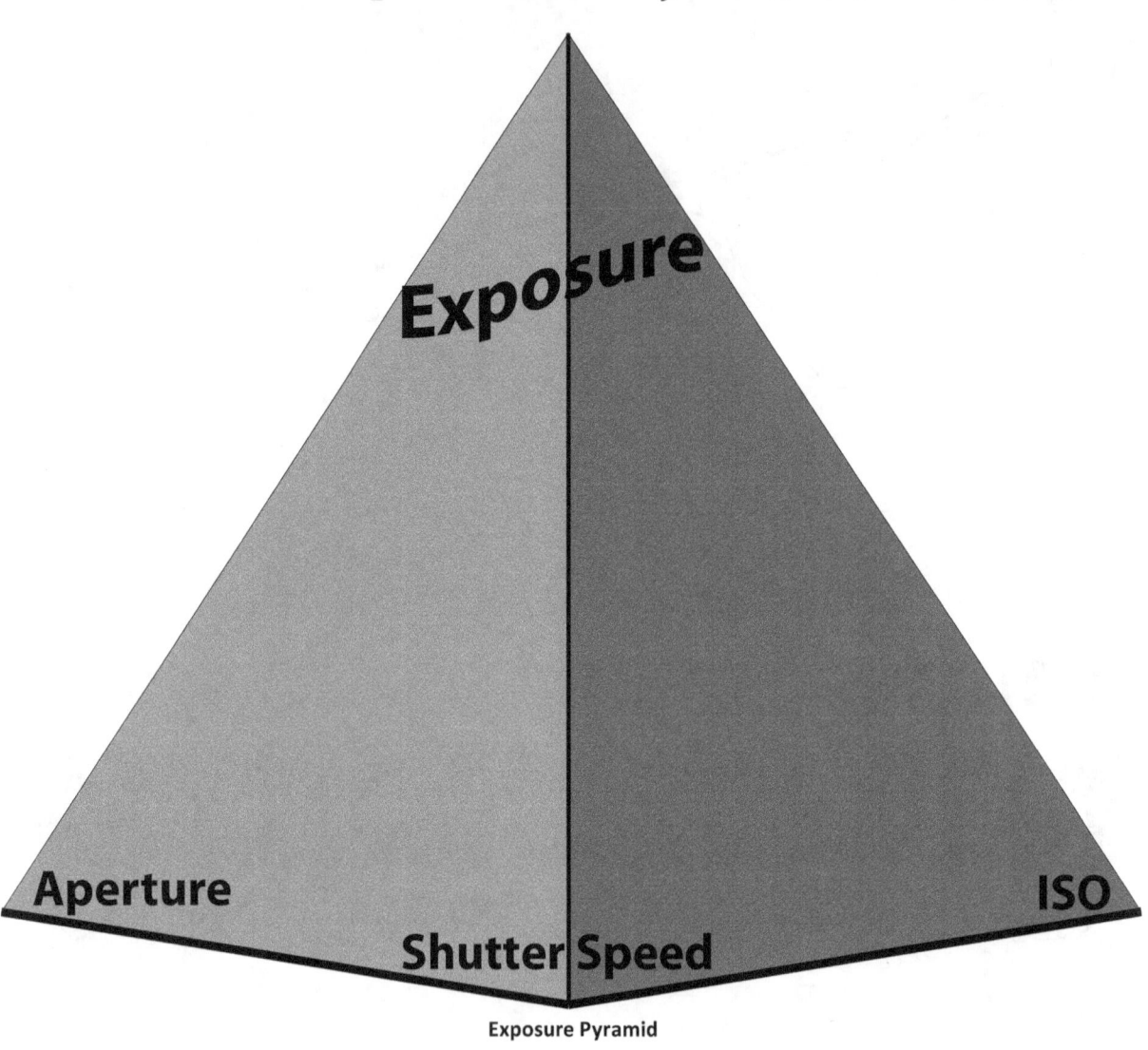
Exposure Pyramid

CAMERA RAW on JPEGS

Adobe Camera RAW is an easy software for making quick adjustments to images shot in RAW. This software can also be used on images shot as JPEGS or scanned as TIFFS. This section is not a tutorial on how to use Adobe Camera Raw, but a tutorial on how to **open** jpeg files with Adobe Camera Raw. The same information for jpeg files applies to TIFF files.

There are two methods of using Adobe's Camera Raw software to open JPEGS, namely, via Adobe Bridge and Adobe Photoshop.

Adobe Bridge

Launch Adobe Bridge.
Navigate to the folder that contains the files you wish to adjust.
Select one or more files (yes, batch processing is allowed).
From the file menu select File, Open in Camera Raw.

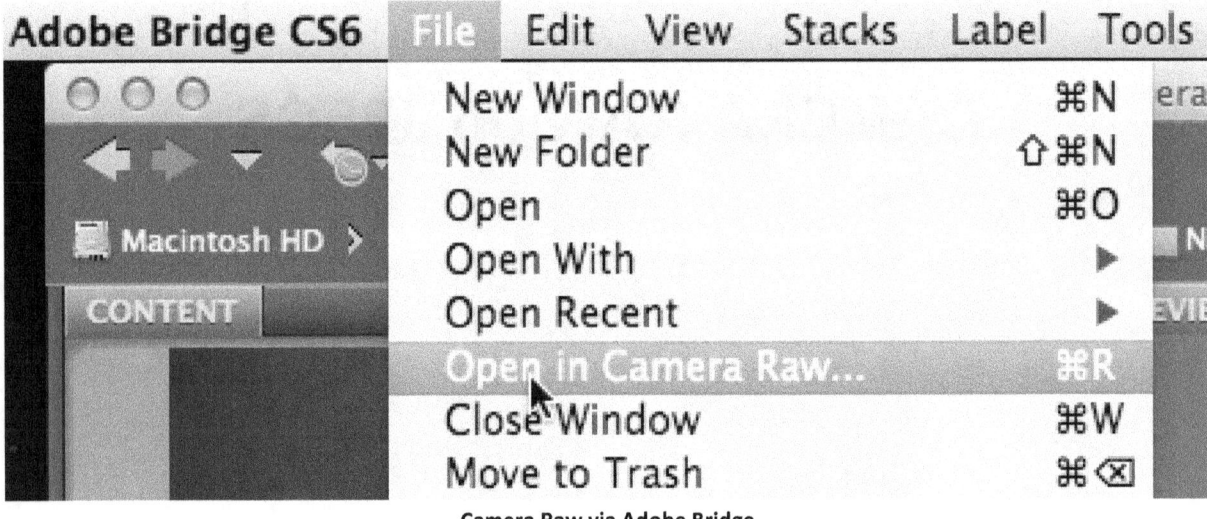

Camera Raw via Adobe Bridge

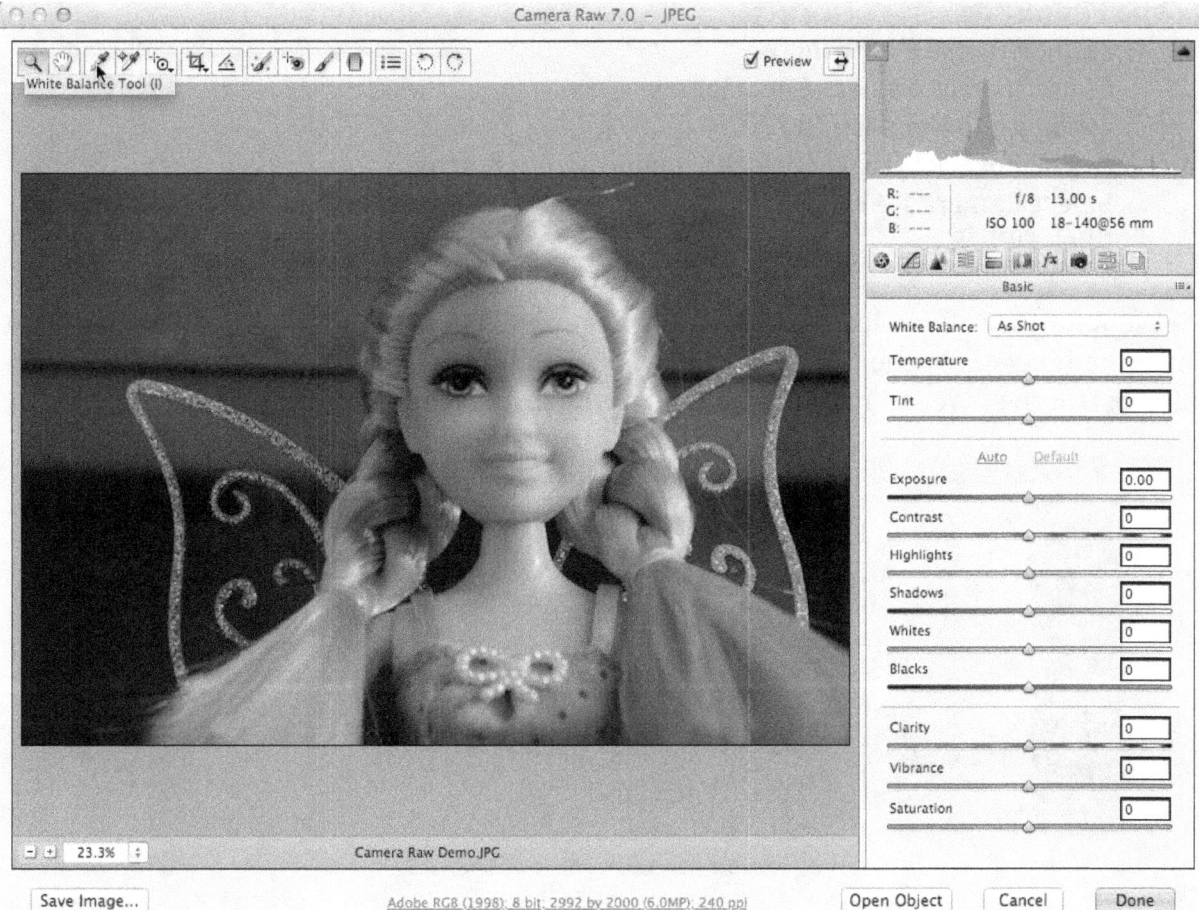

Camera Raw and White Balance

White Balance, for example, can be adjusted by selecting the White Balance Tool at the top left of the screen (beside the hand). Next, pick a color in your photograph that represents what the white balance should be (like the sliver wings). The image will change to reflect the new white balance. Other options for changing white balance is on the right side of the screen where "White Balance: As Shot" can be replaced with "Auto" or "Custom". If "Custom" is selected then an adjustment to the Temperature and Tint changes the white balance. If you adjust the Temperature and Tint before selecting "Custom" then the software will default to Custom.

Adobe Photoshop
    Launch Adobe Photoshop.
    From the menu select File, Open.
    Navigate to the desired file.
    At the Format: JPEG, click the double arrow button.
    Select Camera RAW.
    Click OPEN.

Please note that all we have done is to change the FORMAT from Jpeg to Camera Raw. Once the image is opened in Photoshop's Camera Raw software, the changes made are non destructive. We are making changes to the jpeg's Meta Data, not to the file.

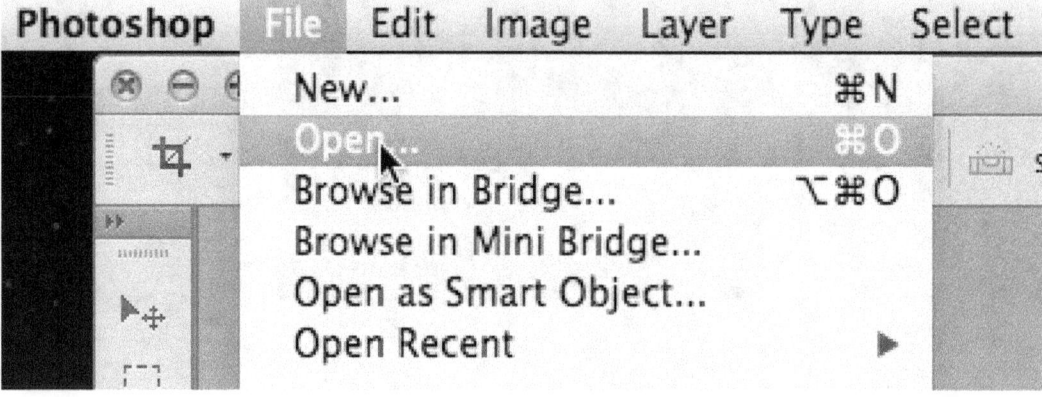

Camera Raw via Adobe Photoshop 1

Camera Raw via Adobe Photoshop 2

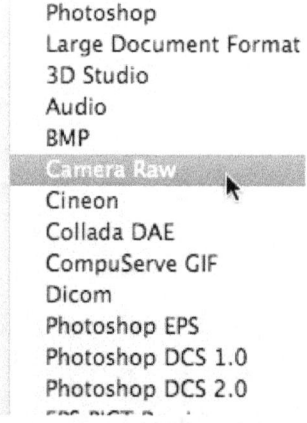

Camera Raw via Adobe Photoshop 3

Notes about Camera Raw
Once you are in Camera Raw there are a few command buttons you need to be aware of.

Open
Open, opens the corrected version in Photo Shop. Once an image is opened in Photoshop you have the option of writing over the original file (**destructive**)

Save Image....
This option saves a copy of the image. The image can be saved in a different file format and with different parameters.

Done:
Done will Close the file but the changes are still in the Meta Data (you are simply saving the meta data).

Option Key
On a MAC, when using Adobe Photoshop or Adobe Bridge, the option key changes the following command buttons:

Open Image becomes **Open Copy**
Cancel becomes **Reset**
Done becomes **Done**
Save Image.... becomes **Save Image**

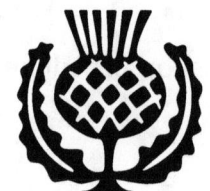

INDEX

A, 6
Adobe Bridge, 180, 183
Adobe Camera RAW, 180
Adobe Photoshop, 180, 183
Aperture, 15-17, 19, 22, 27, 35, 37, 42, 60, 65, 78-81, 83-85, 88, 142, 145, 172, 174-178
Aperture Priority, 7, 20-21, 25-26, 60, 88, 172
Aperture Priority Mode, 19
APS-C, 168-169
APS-H, 168
Area, 16
Aspect Ratio, 157-160, 164, 166
Assignments, 7
Automatic Mode, 60
Blur, 33-35, 145
Bokeh, 17
Bracketing, 11, 13, 88, 99-100, 103-105, 107-108
Bulb, 150-151, 153-154
Camera, 60
Camera Raw, 182
Camera Raw on JPEGS, 179
Canon 1D Mark IV, 168
Canon EOS 600D, 168
Canon G1, 168
Casio EX-Z1200, 168
Center weighted, 12, 14
Center-weighted metering, 10
Cloudy, 125, 129
Control Panel, 37
Correct Exposure, 143, 145
Crop, 158, 160-165, 169
Crop factor, 169
Crop to size, 164
Curtain, 32
Depth of Field, 16, 80
Destructive, 183
Digital Single Lens Reflex, 169
Direct Sunlight, 125, 129
dSLR, 64, 169
EV, 78, 80, 88, 101-102
EV Line graph, 92
Exposure, 6-7, 10, 60, 64, 77-78, 83-85, 88, 94, 143, 149, 151, 173-174, 176, 178
Exposure Compensation, 11, 13, 48, 87-90, 94-95, 100, 112-113, 172
Exposure Histograms, 112

Exposure Pyramid, 78, 178
Exposure Value, 78, 80, 88
Exposure Value Line, 80
Fast Shutter Speed, 33
Fit in frame, 164-165
Flash, 125, 129
Flood light, 32
Fluorescent, 125, 129
Fluorescent light, 124
F-Number, 16, 145
Focal length, 17, 19-20, 34, 169
Focus, 17
Freeze, 33-35, 145
F-stops, 16, 18
Fujifilm FinePix X20, 168
Full Frame, 168-169
Full Stops, 18
Gray Paper, 135
HDR, 102
High Dynamic Range, 102
Histogram, 88, 111-116, 118-120, 172
Image Quality, 8
Incandescent, 124, 129, 134
Index, 185
Introduction, 5
ISO, 6-7, 38, 43, 48, 53, 60, 64-65, 67-69, 73, 78, 80, 172, 174, 176, 178
ISO Sensitivity, 63, 66, 71-72
JPEGS, 179-180, 182
(K), 124
Kelvin, 124
LCD, 37
Lens, 16-17, 19-20
Light, 6, 10, 16, 32, 38, 42, 64-65, 78-83, 124, 134, 168, 171-172, 176-178
Light Value, 78
Long Exposure, 149, 151-152, 154-155
LV, 78
M, 6, 142
Manual, 7, 88, 142, 150
Manual Exposure, 142
Manual Mode, 141, 143-147
MAPS, 6, 19, 37, 60, 142
MAPS Diagram, 7
Matrix, 12, 14
Matrix metering, 10
Mercury-Vapor, 124

Meter, 142
Metering, 9-14
Micro Four Thirds, 168
Nikkor, 19
Nikon d800, 168
Non Destructive, 182
Olympus Pen E-PL5, 168
Opening up, 16
Optimal Exposure, 88
Overexposed, 35, 48, 51, 88, 91-92, 96, 105, 109, 112-113, 142, 150, 178
P, 6, 60
Pentax Q, 168
Photograph, 6
Photographer, 60
Program, 88
Program Mode, 7, 59-62
RAW, 180
RGB Histogram, 112
S, 6, 37
Sensor, 78, 168
Sensor Size, 167-168, 170, 172
Series, 100
Shade, 125, 129
Shallow Aperture, 35, 145
Shutter, 32, 65, 150, 173-174, 177
Shutter Priority, 37-39, 43-44, 48-49, 53-54
Shutter Speed, 7, 19, 31-34, 36-37, 42, 60, 78-80, 82-85, 88, 142, 150, 153-154, 156, 173-176, 178
Shutter Speed Priority, 60, 88, 172
Shutter Speeds, 40, 45, 50, 55
Slow Shutter Speed, 33
Sony RX 1, 168
Sony RX100, 168-169
Speed, 36, 173-174
Spot, 12, 14
Spot metering, 10
Stairs Diagram, 16, 18, 24, 81, 83-85
Stepping down, 16
Stopping down, 16, 18
Stretch to fit, 164-165
Sunlight, 124, 134
Telephoto, 17, 34
Temperature scale, 124
Texture, 66
TIFFS, 180

Time, 36, 150-151, 154, 156, 173-174
Tonal range, 112
Tones, 113
Tools needed, 8
Underexposed, 35, 38, 41, 43, 53, 88, 91-92, 96, 105, 109, 112-113, 142, 178
White Balance, 60, 123-127, 129-131, 133-139, 172, 181
White Balance Card, 134
Wide Angle, 17
Wide Open, 17
Width:Height, 158
Windshield wipers, 33
X-axis, 80
Y-axis, 80
Zero, 142-143, 145